DID I REALLY DO THAT?

An Autobiography

BY

Garry Willmott

And in the Beginning	3
Bicycles	13
Get a Job Son	23
MSA	33
SE.Asia	36
Let's Start a Business	44
SEX	47
What Happens in Vegas Stays in Vegas	48
The Apple Isle	54
The Concerts	59
philanthropy	61
Project Management Plan and Overview	67
Stakeholder Roles and Responsibilities	68
Paperback Writer	71
Operation Garry	84
Family History	88

AND IN THE BEGINNING

Chapter 1

HOW IT ALL STARTED.

TUESDAY JANUARY 1, 1952
THE MELBOURNE SUN
BABY STOPPED MOTHER'S FUN

Mrs Vida Willmott of Brighton went to a New Years Eve party with a group of friends but she did not stay till the end. At 11 o'clock Mr Willmott drove his wife to hospital and at 12.15 their son Garry was born.

Mr Willmott returned to the party and the guests "wet the baby's head".

I was the first baby born in 1952.

It was quite an eventful start to an interesting life.

Although my mother never believed it, I remember one event as a baby.

I was in a cot in my parents' bedroom while they entertained friends in the lounge room. I could hear the chatter and laughter and was upset that I was separated from my parents. I cried and cried until finally my mother gave me the ugliest doll I had ever seen. Not that I had seen many at that stage in my life… This made me cry even louder. I don't remember the end result.

CHERRY RIPE

The next significant episode in my life was when my father, an electrician who had been First Officer on the *Duntroon* during the war and spent an additional three years after at sea, took me out on a job when I was four years old. It was Mother's Day and Dad called into a local milk bar to purchase two Cherry Ripes; one for me and one for my mum.

I ate the first Cherry Ripe and soon later asked Dad whether Mum would mind if I took a bite out of her Mother's Day present. He agreed she wouldn't, and this continued until the second Cherry Ripe had been totally consumed by me.

Soon after, I attended Bentleigh Kindergarten. It was located under the Bentleigh Football Stand.

Bentleigh Rec

It was here I met Ian Jones who became my lifelong friend. We still talk once a week. Not many people have maintained such a strong friendship for sixty-seven years and still going.

We used to pinch the rich kids' bikes and ride them around the oval.

The next step up the academic ladder was "Bubs" at Bentleigh West State School.

Mum took me into the classroom where most of the other kids were already seated. I was very nervous until I saw Ian wave at me indicating he had saved a desk next to him. All was well.

As we progressed to 1st grade we joined the Garry Bulch gang. Ian and I were part of the upper echelon of the gang. We weren't exactly the Hells Angles but we did demand respect.

We were also part of the drum band, which drummed the students into class.

1960

After four years at Bentleigh West, I transferred to Haileybury College, one of Melbourne's better schools. My elder brother John had also attended Haileybury six years before me.

The other major event in 1960 was when my parents bought a block of land at 36 Silver Leaves Avenue on Phillip Island. The block next door belonged to our great friends the Jennings family. The children are still close.

The two families built holiday houses and we had the most fantastic times.

Cowes was a wonderful destination; our family spent every weekend at Silver Leaves during the summer months and every second weekend during the rest of the year.

The parents of all the kids would get together in the various houses partying and the kids would get together in another house getting up to mischief.

The front of No 36 Silver Leaves

Us kids would walk into Cowes and go to the Cowes flicks. Elvis was popular as were the westerns. The seats were old bus seats and canvas chairs. Jaffas were the lolly of choice; not only for eating but also for rolling down the aisle.

John and I were given horses by Mum and Dad as we had both shown interest in riding.

John's horse was named Sultan and was a gentle giant who could jump.

My horse was a chestnut pony named Star. She had a terrible temperament.

We built a corral on the back of the block, so we had easy access. The rest of the time they were on a large paddock on the local farm.

The other luxury at Cowes was a speedboat called *Scamp*. It was fast and perfect for water skiing.

I had access to *Scamp* from the age of thirteen and I became a proficient sailor.

When I was sixteen, Ian and another friend, John, and I were allowed to stay at Silver Leaves by ourselves.

We decided to take *Scamp* into town where I would drop the boys off beside the pier. They had my clothes in a plastic bag. The plan was for me to take *Scamp* out from the shore and swim back.

I ripped *Scamp* at full tilt, turning at the pier but the engine seized. I pulled it up only to find fishing line tangled around the propeller.

I heard some fellow yelling and threatening me.

Ian and John were on the pier during this unfortunate occurrence. Apparently this fellow was calmly fishing when my prop ripped the fishing rod out of his hands. It went sailing through the air.

Fortunately a kid on the pier dived in and rescued the fishing rod. All was forgiven. It was back to the original plan underage drinking at the pub. I swam out to *Scamp* and backed her into the beach, so Ian and John didn't need to get their feet wet. A quick trip back to our mooring again and I dropped the two spoiled friends back on the beach and moored the boat then I swam back to the beach. It seems I got the rough end of the pineapple.

My father, Sam, suffered from chronic arthritis. The doctors were injecting him with gold. He was advised to move to a warmer climate, so they moved to the Gold Coast in Queensland.

They sold the family homes in Bentleigh and Cowes. They sold McKittick Road for $28,000; the most recent figure for the site was $1,500,000. It was a beautiful home, but developers knocked it down and built two townhouses. Silver Leaves' most current value is $1,000,000 but they sold it for $11,000.

Sam left his business to his son John to manage but unfortunately Dad was forced to liquidate the business after only a year after handing over the reins. What happened? I don't know.

McKittrick Road plus Sophie

Now 8a & 8b McKittrick Road Value 1,700,000 each

School Days

Chapter 2

The most significant event at Haileybury was my cheekiness award. Mr Pugh the Religious teacher walked onto the oval and unrolled a scroll. He pronounced that no rough games could be played including British Bulldog. The list was rather long.

I asked him if we could play "drop the hankie". This infuriated him and he ordered me to the headmaster's office.

While waiting outside Mr Cornish's office I heard the end of lunch bell ring fifteen minutes early. I was told to go to the main assembly hall.

The headmaster gave a stern lecture about being cheeky to teachers. He announced that the boy who perpetrated the latest crime would be caned severely. At this stage I felt slightly uncomfortable. At the end of the assembly I was required to return to the headmaster's office to receive my punishment.

I couldn't believe the pain.

I left Haileybury after year seven and attended Moorabbin Technical College as my brother had done before me.

I had several fights that first day but fortunately I won all of them. Having had a few years doing Judo helped. I earned the respect from the roughnecks.

It was a rough school, and I received the strap on a regular basis.

On a more positive note I topped the 4th and 5th year.

I was also school swimming captain the first year Moorabbin won the inter school swimming title. I was school swimming champion for all the years I attended Moorabbin.

Ian and I were invited to stay at Sandy Camp Quambone NSW by the station managers who were staying with family friends at Phillip Island. Our parents agreed and we were soon jackerooing. The drought had just broken and there was water everywhere. It was also very cold which was unusual.

Ian and I stayed in the jackeroos' quarters, which were rudimentary to say the least. There were no windows; just flywire so the freezing wind would whistle through lifting the blankets above the bed and exposing our freezing sixteen-year-old bodies.

The mustering sheds were fifty kilometres from the homestead and once we arrived there we were each allocated a horse. We then began mustering about two hundred head at a time along the Darling River and beyond. Our stay at Sandy Camp was amazing. What wasn't amazing was eating mutton every night.

THE SHARPIE ERA

The sharpies dressed well and sported short haircuts. On the surface every mother would love them. Their looks were deceptive for they were in fact street gangs who practised severe violence against innocent people.

I was returning from a dance in South Yarra with a few mates. We were walking up the Moorabbin station ramp when two sharpies walked onto the top of the ramp and stood either side. The one they called Whippy hit me in the face. I don't remember fighting him but what I do remember is seeing him unconscious on the ramp.

My good friend dispatched the other one.

We continued on our way until about thirty sharpies confronted us. The leader had a sawn-off shotgun. He informed me he intended to shoot me.

I took off at great speed and decided I needed to stay off the streets. I climbed over backyard fence after backyard fence. I covered a couple of kilometres using this stealth method. I finally made it home safely. I was told the thugs were cruising the street in a black Ford intent on shooting me.

Ironically, I was attending a local dance the following week. I was waiting in line when Whippy approached me and asked for 20 cents. The idiot didn't recognise me I said no. I arranged for a group of mates to follow me when we left the dance. There was no trouble, but another guy got glassed.

I completed secondary school and then stayed on at Moorabbin and completed the first year of my Business Studies Diploma.

There were only twelve students, and we had a ball apart from the study.

One significant event was the first moonwalk. My parents were away travelling somewhere so I invited the class to watch it at my place. We bought some beer and settled in for the event of a lifetime. We weren't disappointed.

The second and subsequent years were at Caulfield Institute of Technology (now Monash University).

Campus life was great fun. One particular event was when Melbourne Tech raided us with flour bombs. We declared revenge and enlisted Swinburne Tech to join us as an ally.

I'm not sure how many of us there were but it could have been a hundred. As we all walked down to the square the Chancellor stopped us with a megaphone.

He implored us to refrain throwing flour bombs and return to our own campuses.

I now must admit it was me that threw the first bomb, hitting the Chancellor on the chest. It then became a free for all. We even attracted a television news channel.

CIT (Caulfield Tech)

BICYCLES

Chapter 3

Life is like riding a bicycle to keep your balance you must keep moving
Albert Einstein

The first bicycle I owned was a hand-me-down from my brother. It was a faded red colour. Excited I hopped aboard the three-wheeler and rode out onto the street. All the wheels fell off as soon as I hit the bitumen. I was devastated.

Dad put me into the Plymouth and drove me to the local bike shop. He purchased s Cyclops three-wheeler, light blue in colour. I went from devastated to elated.

My New Bike

The next level up was a 24-inch Malvern Star. I covered many kilometres on that little speedster.

The final step was a 28-inch street-racing bike. This bike took me many kilometres around Melbourne.

A friend and neighbour was a guy called Noel Parsons. He was a very bright guy; in fact he became Dux of the school every year. Noel completed a degree in Chemistry Engineering and ended up CEO of a chemical company.

Once a year Noel and I would ride our bikes from Bentleigh to Mt Eliza; a total of 80 kilometres.

The Beginning of Oliver's Hill

Towards the end of the journey we were required to climb Oliver's Hill; a six-kilometre climb. Coming down was much more fun.

The final ride we undertook together was when we experienced a sight which was truly amazing.

As we were descending we came across several cars parked on the side of the road. We braked and asked a motorist what was going on. He didn't answer us. He just pointed to the sky.

Noel and I couldn't believe it when we saw a cigar-shaped silver object. It disappeared in an instant. We told our parents when we arrived back home and they believed us. There was a TV report that night.

Another episode happened soon after when three very wealthy businessmen who were friends of my parents were driving to Mr Smith's luxury holiday house on Silver Leaves Avenue. My parents were waiting in the house to join the three for dinner.

As the men were driving past a small town called Yass they noticed a UFO following them above the macrocarpa tree line. When they arrived at the house they were shaking. They had no doubt as to what they saw.

SURFING

This photo was taken at Wilson's Promontory. I'm the one lying down amongst the squalor.

It was meeting a few new friends at Caulfield that got me into surfing. Soon I was hooked. I borrowed money from my parents and bought a 1964 Kombi Van. My brother, John created a bed with storage underneath and installed a shelf along the back of the front seat. He installed a gas stove and fabricated a steel bull bar on the front. John was very clever with his hands.

Me @ 20

Judging by the Boards we had 5 in the van

I was able to arrange my lectures to be attended Monday through to Thursday, giving my mates and me a long weekend to go surfing.

The surf beach we most frequented was Bells Beach.

Bells with surfable waves

Bells unsurfable for me

The most memorable time I had at Bells was also one of the scariest. We pulled up at the Bells car park on top of the cliff. Actually it was hardly a car park. We hopped out of the Kombi and observed the waves. They were medium size; certainly within our skill level. We suited up and made the rough descent to the beach. We were catching 6 to 8 foot waves, which is about the perfect size wave at Bells. Gradually we noticed the waves were getting bigger and bigger and within an hour and a half of entering the surf the waves had reached twenty feet.

Funeral for my surfboard

We all spent the next hour trying to avoid being smashed. Finally I reached the eight-foot shore break but unfortunately a wave broke my board in half.

Another scary event while surfing was at Winki Pop, the break next to Bells Beach. I got caught in a rip, which was taking me into a ferocious blowhole. I was paddling as hard as I could, but I was not making any headway. If I entered the blowhole I would have been smashed against the cave wall, which would have killed me. Just as I was about to abandon my surfboard and swim, I discovered a channel to get me out.

One of the highlights of the surfing weekends away was going to the pub and listening to various bands. On one particular occasion we went to the Lorne Hotel. I don't recall what band was playing. It could have been Max Merritt. They were finishing their gig when I started playing the drums on the table. I just went into a trance, playing my heart out for quite some time. I finally stopped and the patrons who had been leaving stopped and began applauding, as did the band. I must admit I felt like Ringo Star.

Another Kombi adventure was when Ian and a guy called Kevin drove to the Gold Coast in 1972. The object was to surf and meet girls. We managed to do both. I ran into a girl from Caulfield Tech called Sharon at the Surfers Paradise beer garden. She was staying on the coast with two girlfriends, Maureen and Kate. I ended up with Kate and she remained my girlfriend for the next two years.

The MOI was for a three-hour drive while the previous driver would sleep in the back on the luxurious bed.

It was my time to sleep just out of Sydney when the other two woke me with the news the cabin had filled with smoke. The engine was now an ex-engine. We pushed it into a service station at Picton and hitchhiked back to Melbourne.

My father arranged for a transport company he dealt with to bring it back, and he wasn't impressed.

It took me some time to save enough to purchase a reconditioned motor.

Needless to say I had some fantastic times surfing, the camaraderie of my mates, smoking dope, meeting chicks and going to the Torquay pub listening to Billy Thorpe and other top bands.

Rest Time

Just before I was injured

The next phase of my life encompassed riding trail bikes through the Victorian bush. A group of mates including my brother would ride on bush tracks and creek beds in an area near Healesville. There was only one injury incurred and it was me who suffered the unfortunate incident. My foot was slammed into the bike having hit a large rock. This created a hole, which required six internal and six external stiches at the Healesville Community Hospital. My fellow riders were pissed off that the weekend had been ruined.

The next stage of my life was when my parents moved to the Gold Coast for my father's health.

They purchased a house four doors down from the house I grew up in. I was the major tenant, which meant finding two other people to share with me. Over a period of twelve months eight flatmates came and went. There were periods when I was the only occupant, which meant most of my $55 weekly pay went to paying the rent. I didn't tell my parents; why I'm not sure— possibly pride.

2 McKittrick Road Bentleigh

I began to feel down, really down. In fact I went to my family doctor, Dr Dyet. He diagnosed me as having clinical depression. My mother flew down from the Gold Coast hoping she could rectify the situation. When she saw me she realised how depressed I was. Her advice was stop taking the anti-depressant pills and take an extended holiday in my Kombi Van, surfing and relaxing.

I took her advice and together with a couple of mates headed up to Queenland. We parked the Kombi just outside Noosa National Park and stayed there for three months, surfing most days.

We then drove up to Cairns and Port Douglas. While we were there we met two American guys who were riding around Australia on 650 Yamahas. We also met a couple of georgous girls. The down side of that was they were infatuated with the Yanks.

GET A JOB SON

Chapter 4

My depression had subsided, and I was feeling pretty good. I had just finished a surf and was sitting on a towel beside the Kombi thinking "what a life" when it suddenly dawned on me.

Is this what I want all my life?
Do I want to marry?
Do I want children?
Do I want a nice house to live in?

The answer to these questions was obvious. YES

I packed up the Kombi and informed everybody I was returning to Melbourne.

When I reached Coolangatta there were several people hitchhiking, I stopped to pick up a guy who looked reasonable, and he turned out to be a good companion for the trip to Melbourne. His name was Dave and although his hometown was Brisbane he was heading for Melbourne; a city he had never been to before.

Dave and I parted ways once we reached my hometown, although I did catch up with him once or twice.

Having studied Business Studies the obvious career to pursue was accounting. I made an appointment with Drake International in Dandenong. The consultant's name was Ben Crocker. He sent me to an interview at a book distribution company owned by Collins. The name of this prestigious company was Collins Forlib.

I got the job as junior accountant but after a year working there I realised, and the company realised I was a terrible accountant.

Back to Drake but this time I made an appointment with their head office.

I explained to the consultant I hated accounting and I wished to find a career that was exciting and at which I could excel. I must have impressed him. He referred me to a more senior consultant who I impressed as well; finally I was introduced to the big boss, Paul Veith.

After five interviews and an IQ test I was offered the position of Account Representative for Dandenong and Doncaster. It was unusual to have two sales areas.

By this stage I had sold my Kombi for more than I originally paid for it and purchased a Holden Premier. I did this to impress my girlfriend, Jan.

The Silver Streak

Jan was my first true love at the age of sixteen. We were both madly in love but after two years she dropped me for a much older man.

Jan aged 16

Jan is far left. Joanna is a family friend hugging me I've known her since I was two.

Me at age 16

It didn't take long to produce the results Paul was hoping for. The minimum age for this position was twenty-five. I had just turned twenty-two and led the sales figures selling temp office workers i.e. *Drake Overload*.

I began at Drake in January 1974 and was promoted to Queensland Branch manager in the following June. Thus my interstate transfers began.

Drake's offices were on the 4th floor of the T&G building. I arrived on Monday morning and began the introduction process. My staff included Mimi, Carol and Wendy. Mimi showed me my office, which included a broken-down desk and chair. My first task was to purchase new office furniture.

The state managers met each quarter at Melbourne's Head Office. It was held over a weekend, and I was looking forward to my first managers' meeting. Unfortunately, my figures were the worst of all the states. The other managers reviewed my branch's performance, which was a humiliating experience. I flew home with my tail between my legs.

The next managers' meeting was held three months later and to my delight Brisbane was rated number one.

I was on my way.

The receptionist was Beth Webster. We had to retrench her as Australia was in a recession at the time. Drake found her a job, which took her interstate selling business magazines.

I asked her out prior to her departing, and she accepted.

She returned three months later. I picked her up from the airport and drove he back to my St Lucia unit. We lived together for seventeen years and had two daughters. In the 17th year she announced she wanted a divorce.

Things continued to go well, and twelve months later Brisbane was the most profitable branch in Australia. I was awarded a $13,500 bonus, which was a significant sum considering my salary was $10,000. The downside was Drake's decision to spread the bonus over five years.

I purchased our first house in Paddington for $22,000 and began to renovate it. By the time we were ready to sell it was valued at $37,000. It didn't sell so we let it out.

It last sold for $2,200,000

I had been headhunted by the General Manager of a computer bureau, which was a subsidiary of TNT. Initially I showed little interest as it meant transferring to Sydney. I changed my mind when I learnt of Drake's five-year bonus decision.

Beth and I had got engaged initially to placate our parents. When we decided to move to Sydney we decided to get married. My closest friend was Ian Jones. He was unable to make it to Brisbane so I asked my brother John to be Best Man, but he refused. I asked John Brodie— a recently made friend— to do the honours, and he accepted.

Once I accepted the Sydney position life became a rollercoaster, we found a tenant, got married and drove to Sydney. Once we arrived we needed to find a place to rent. Not knowing Sydney very well we chose 1940s renovated unit in the very posh suburb of Bellevue Hill.

We had a first-floor unit

It didn't take long for Beth and me to make new friends. Beth secured a PA position with a director of IBM and made many friends in the company.

I worked with an amazing group of people both male and female. We all worked hard but we also played hard.

Mum and Dad were keen to invest in Sydney property in partnership with us. We purchased a semi-detached in Woollahra for $44,000. After I accepted the Adelaide position the bank insisted I sell Woollahra or Paddington. We were forced to sell for $55,000.

TNT paid all my selling costs, so we sold It. I have never forgiven Westpac.

Valued at $3,400,000 2023

It didn't take long to settle into TNT Paycost. My biggest achievement was signing ITCorp, which became the biggest sale TNT had ever made. The commission was huge but that's another story. Citicorp called me the day after my first meeting and signed up Tasmania as a trial.

Soon after I was approached by the General Manager to determine if I would accept the South Australian manager's role. I accepted and he gave me three months to sign Citicorp.

It turned out to be six months and I received nothing. There seemed to be a trend of not receiving bonuses or commissions.

Just before we made the move to Adelaide I purchased my father's car, which he'd bought it in London. It was a Toyota Crown two-door coupe. There were only six in Australia.

I paid $4000 and sold it for $5,000 today's value is $1,300,000 it's a very rare motor vehicle.

We enjoyed living in Adelaide where we made lots of friends and made many excursions to the Barossa and Clare Valleys.

There was a downside; my bipolar kicked in with extreme depression. There was no particular reason. I was due to travel to Sydney for a management meeting. I was paranoid about attending because I was sure I was going to be sacked.

I was so bad the company flew me back to Adelaide in the company of a nurse.

I was on sick leave for four weeks. When I returned I was in my manic phase when I could achieve anything.

It was in Adelaide that I began to take golf seriously, not necessarily skilfully but seriously.

DARWIN

TNT leased a Lear Jet to fly courier bags to Darwin stopping in Alice Springs and Tennant Creek along the way.

I was offered a seat to endeavour to break open the Darwin market. All in all I flew on the jet a dozen times. It wasn't exactly luxury. I slept on top of the courier bags most of the time.

I was successful in signing up several government departments plus the university.

I had a number of interesting experiences. The day Lindy Chamberlain was found guilty for killing Azaria, her baby, I had dinner with two of the jury members who worked for a client TIO insurance a government owned insurance company. The judge joined us all. They were of course convinced of her guilt. The law is an ass.

Another experience was when I was eating dinner in the Darwin Hotel restaurant. I ordered steak and perused the wine list for a wine to accompany it.

What stood out was a Grange Hermitage 1970 for $15. I eagerly ordered a bottle. The publican approached me and inquired if I would be interested in purchasing his stock. His reason was that red wine was unpopular in Darwin.

He offered me 24 bottles at $7.00 a bottle. I agreed and took possession of the classic wine.

Today the vintage retails for $1000 a bottle.

I loaded the precious cargo on the Lear Jet and off we went. Just as we took off from Tennant Creek an alarm sounded, and extremely hot air poured into the cabin. I could hear *pop, pop* and thinking the worst I was distraught.

Back in Adelaide I cellared the Grange hoping it wasn't ruined. After three months I cracked a bottle; it was just as perfect as the bottle I had in Darwin.

I drank the rest over a couple of years, sharing with my family and friends.

MSA

Southern Drawl

Chapter 5

1980

I decided it was time to leave TNT Payroll. Working in England appealed so I wrote to a few software companies.

A company in Sydney of all places approached me. The company was MSA. Their VP in Europe was impressed with my application, but he thought I would be more suitable for Australia.

The Sales Manager flew me from Adelaide to Sydney and together with their top salesman interviewed me. I passed the test; the next step was getting the tick from the Managing Director, Judith Lightfoot. She hired me for Adelaide and Perth. Based in Sydney, I was on a plane every week. This schedule put my marriage under strain.

Management Science America (MSA) was the largest software company in the world at the time. It released a new version (21) of its general ledger system just as I joined the company. It was a disaster. It was infested with bugs, and sales dropped dramatically around the globe.

My first trip to head office in Atlanta was a humbling experience I was at the bottom of the sales ladder.

Despite this Judith allowed me to fly to England, France and Hong Kong. She had faith in my ability.

I did not sell a system in my first year but once the software issues were rectified I sold over $1,000,000 making me one of the top 10% of salesmen in the world.

You would have thought all things were good. Not so, a new sales manager was appointed from head office in Atlanta. He and I clashed.

I left the company and joined their main competitor, Software International.

1983

The most significant event was welcoming our first daughter into the world. Emma Louise was born on the 3rd of July.

1984

The three of us moved to Maleny and our renovated Queenslander.

1985

Our second daughter Sophie Jane was born on 15th December at Nambour hospital.

My first year with SI was spent selling in Melbourne and Queensland.

Danny, Chris, Steve and me off to dinner and Wankity Wanks.

I wrote the script and acted as host of the parody of Blankity Blanks, a popular TV show. The plastic bags carried our costumes.

Another significant event in that year was moving from Brisbane to Maleny in the hinterland of the Sunshine Coast.

It wasn't a simple move. It encompassed cutting an 1890s colonial house in half and moving it one hundred miles and restoring it.

Maleny Renovated

I convinced the General Manager that I could operate from home efficiently despite Maleny being one and a half hours from Brisbane airport.

Maleny Early Days of Renovation

S.E. Asia

Chapter 6

In 1983 I was appointed Sales Director for S.E. Asia, which meant I was in Asia for two weeks of every month. This was very hard on my family.

During the four years I held that position, I travelled thirty-five times to Singapore, Malaysia. Thailand and Indonesia.

I and another colleague were invited to tour the Indonesian Government's aircraft factory in Bandung about an hour from Jakarta. The General Manager was Mr Habibie, a very nice gentleman. He provided us with a delicious lunch and then bade us goodbye once we had completed the tour.

The following year he became President of Indonesia.

I had only the one visit to Brunei with the invitation of the Government. I was asked to present our software to the Brunei Treasury. Brunei does not have an Embassy in Australia however; my treasury contact suggested we would receive our visa at the immigration desk upon arrival.

There were three of us when we asked for our visas. The immigration officer had no knowledge of any arrangement made with Treasury and there were certainly no visas waiting for us.

We were escorted by two armed officers into a small room and told to sit quietly. We did as we were told; the officers were holding automatic assault rifles.

We decided to ask if we could purchase visas. The answer was yes. However another problem presented itself. We had to pay in Brunei Dollars, we were only carrying US Dollars based on the advice given to us by our travel agent.

My colleague, Peter, asked if he could enter the terminal and change the US dollars into Brunei Dollars. The guards agreed and after fifteen minutes Peter returned smiling like a Cheshire cat. Apparently the money exchange was closed but he heard an Australian accent and approached a very distinguished gentleman who agreed to exchange the currency.

There was just one problem. Peter's maths was not very good. He exchanged cash for two people and there was three of us. I volunteered to exchange the additional cash. Peter told me the gentleman was about to board a large black limousine. I spotted him and approached, explaining my predicament. He couldn't exchange but could give me the Brunei currency if we agreed to pay him at his hotel, the same hotel where we were staying. He gave me his business card. His name was Viscount Slim.

Mark William Rawdon Slim, 3rd Viscount Slim (born 13 February 1960), is the **son of the 2nd Viscount and his wife Elisabeth Joan Spinney**. *He was educated at Eton College and the University of Bristol and in 2003 was using an address at 15 Basinghall Street in the City of London.*

I returned to the group, and we were able to purchase three visas and allowed to depart, catching a taxi to the hotel.

We caught up with Viscount Slim and paid him the money we owed him. He invited us to join his group and we enjoyed the rest of the evening.

Another interesting event was staying in Bangkok when the army committed a coup in 1981. The army had soldiers on every major street corner as well as tanks rolling down the main roads. The navy were patrolling the Chao Phraya river.

The population were advised to stay off the street.

I was in the men's rest room of the Oriental Hotel when several soldiers stormed in taking some poor fellow with them when they departed. I decided it would be best to get out of Bangkok ASAP. When I arrived at the airport and tried to check-in I discovered a Thai General had seconded my ticket. I had to wait two days before I could get out.

In Bangkok we stayed initially at the Hilton Hotel. Peter and I were amongst the first guests at the hotel and were invited to attend its grand opening. It certainly was a grand affair with several hundred people attending. We met and conversed with the Australian Ambassador and various other dignitaries.

I required the services of the hotel's business centre to type a proposal to Thai International. A beautiful young woman called Noy managed the centre. She did a great job for me, and I rewarded her with an expensive box of Belgian chocolates. We got to know one another and she invited me home for a meal and to meet her husband who was a Lieutenant Colonel in the army.

It wasn't long after that when I received an invitation for dinner at Noy's uncle's residence. He was a prince. He was one of three princes in the Royal Family and therefore, an elite royal.

Noy and her husband drove me to the prince's penthouse, located in a klong off Sukhumvit, one of Bangkok's main roads.

He was very gracious, welcoming me to his large and opulent apartment. The banquet was magnificent; I noticed a putting green on his large balcony, and he challenged me to a putting competition. I accepted knowing full well I would lose. You don't beat the prince.

After a very pleasant evening was had by all we bade the prince farewell. We drove up to the intersection and amazingly two policemen stopped the traffic so we could turn into one of the busiest roads in Bangkok.

I experienced both good and bad in Bangkok. One of the bad experiences was when Peter and I needed to use an air bridge between a department store and an office tower where we had a business appointment. Access to the bridge was via the pet floor where we were flabbergasted to see caged lions, tigers, cobras and pythons all for sale.

I had mixed experiences with our Chinese agents.

I had been working on selling Thai Airlines a significant amount of software over a twelve-month period. A group of very senior managers travelled to Australia to visit some of our sites including Qantas. They were about to sign a contract when they decided they would like to visit Singapore Airlines. It was very short notice, and I was committed elsewhere. I requested our agent to accompany them.

He decided it was not in his best interests and stood them up. They were naturally offended and signed with a competitor.

Our agent was castigated severely by our General Manager.

Soon after the agent requested I bring a *Playboy* into Malaysia for him. I reluctantly agreed.

When I arrived at customs they searched my briefcase but alas, couldn't find the magazine.

The agent had set me up; if they had found the magazine I would have received a jail sentence.

Sukhumvit

For some unknown reason I was regarded as handsome in Thailand. I asked Noy why this was so. She explained there was only one guest who had stayed at the Hilton who was more handsome than me.

I must admit I was chuffed. Peter couldn't get over some girl in the street coming up to me and saying Khuṇ hĺx. *You are beautiful.*

Yeah, I know it hasn't happened anywhere else in the world and is not likely to.

The managing director of Software International, Steve, was a complex individual. The sales team from Australia approached the president of the company when we visited Andover in Massachusetts requesting he be dismissed. Unfortunately the president was organising a management buyout and Steve was an integral part of the plan.

An example of Steve's management style was when I wrote him a memo while he was in the USA. The subject was to perform some modifications to some software. The change was fairly simple but if agreed we would sell a significant amount of software to Malaysian Airways. Not only that, but we would be replacing our major competitor MSA. My secretary suggested that I copy in the president. I achieved my objective. The modifications were agreed, and I got the sale. Steve didn't speak to me for a year.

We would have seminars each year in the various countries. Presentations would be made by various product specialists. The night before the seminar in Malaysia, Steve assigned me the task of presenting Fixed Assets; something I had never done before. He was hoping it would trip me up.

I took the slide carousel back to my room and began rehearsing. When it came for my presentation I was extremely nervous. I got through it and was rated by the audience as the best presentation. Steve was livid.

It was inevitable that Steve was never going to forgive me for what he perceived as going behind his back so I decided to leave the company. I had led a group of Indonesian companies on a tour of Australian companies using the Software International financial applications. They were interested in supply and plant maintenance applications which Software International didn't have. I did some research and discovered a Brisbane company that specialised in the applications. The company was called Mincom.

The Indonesians were impressed with the company's products and I was impressed with the company. I approached David Merson, the founder and Managing Director, to ascertain if he would be interested in hiring me.

After a few interviews they hired me as their first National Sales Manager. I was a NSM without any senior sales people. I hired salesmen in New South Wales and Victoria and began the task of rebadging the look and feel of the company.

I achieved significant sales growth over the next three years.

An example of a successful sale was Newcrest Mining, one of Australia's biggest gold mining companies. Recent output has been 2,100,000 ounces of gold in one year.

In a meeting with the Company Secretary, Gary Scanlon, in the Melbourne head office I was told we were behind in our bid to our biggest competitor. The reason was we were more expensive. I sharpened my pencil, and we were back in the race. Four colleagues and I flew in a ten-seater plane to Telfer mine in the Great Sandy Desert for two days of final presentations.

Open Cut Telfer

At the end of the second day we all met at the Telfer Pub. I asked Gary what he would like to drink. He responded with Chivas Regal whisky. I responded by saying I only bought Chivas Regal for Mincom clients. He looked me in the eye and requested Chivas Regal. That was it; we had won a very large contract.

The plane we flew in crashed the following week on its way to Kalgoorlie killing ten people in all.

Although I travelled around Australia extensively for the company, I only travelled internationally twice, and that was to Papua New Guinea. I travelled there to present our software to the Post Office. It was a successful trip and to celebrate our success I and another Mincom consultant, David, decided to eat dinner at the yacht club and indulge in a few ales. At about 10 pm I decided to walk home to the Travelodge Hotel, a journey of approximately one and a half kilometres. David decided to stay on for a while.

There were no dramas during the journey and I slipped into bed for a restful sleep.

We met in the boardroom next morning and the evaluation team of eight; seven from PNG and an English project manager, asked about our evening. When I informed them of my lone walk back to the hotel they were all horrified.

Apparently packs of 'Rascals' as they were called roamed Port Moresby streets at night looking for easy prey. There was a very high murder rate. They made it clear that I should regard myself as very lucky.

Let's Start a Business

Chapter 7

Peter Simmons was the person who hired me for both MSA and Software International and we were very close. We also lived one street apart in Kenmore Hills, Brisbane. Peter and I travelled extensively in S.E. Asia. We often discussed the concept of establishing a business together.

He suggested he hire me for the third time as he was General Manager of an Australian software company called Paxus. It would give us more time together planning our venture. I agreed and handed my resignation into Mincom. Mincom tried to talk me out of it but I had made up my mind.

I had only just taken up my role as Marketing Manager when I received a unwelcome knock on the door.

On Boxing Day my wife, Beth, was out shopping and I was looking after my two daughters Emma and Sophie. We were eating Cheezels when I picked one up and it felt like silk gradually my body went numb right up to my tongue. I knew I needed to see a doctor. I explained to the girls that I needed to see a doctor and told them not to let anybody in.

The doctor suggested it wasn't too much to worry about but said if it happened again to let him know.

We attended a New Year's Eve party at some friends' house and the numbness occurred again. Now I knew something was up. I made an appointment with my regular doctor on the 2nd and he booked me in for a CAT Scan.

I brought the X-rays back to the surgery and the doctor placed them on the light screen. We looked at each other.

He referred me to a neurosurgeon called James Smith. He advised me he needed to operate as soon as possible. I was wheeled into the operating theatre on the 8th of January. I woke in the ICU eight hours later. I stayed in hospital for two weeks and then recovered at home for a further eight weeks.

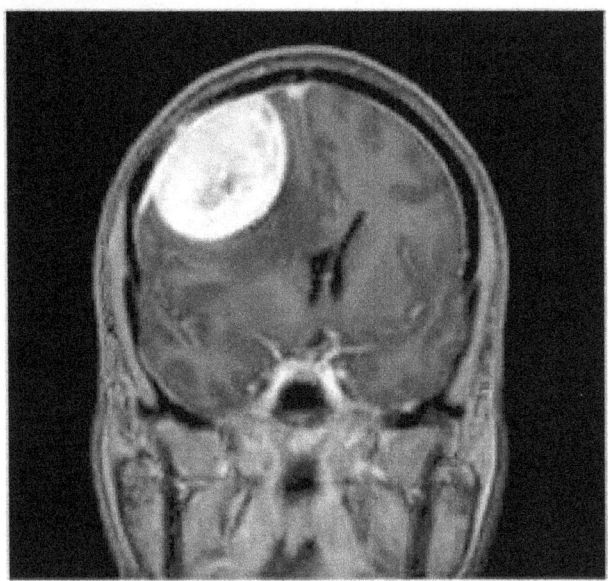

Meningioma

Nine weeks later I was back at work at Paxus. It wasn't a great restart as I was instructed to retrench twenty staff. Then came the news head office would be moving to Sydney. I was given a generous retrenchment package. I thought this would aid Peter and me to start the new venture. What I wasn't aware of was Peter had gone behind my back and signed up with an American company. He had the audacity to offer me a position with his company. I refused his offer.

The irony of it all was the woman he appointed in my place embezzled a large sum of money, forcing Peter to close down the company.

I created my own company called Future Directions, selling a number of packages including Occupational Health and Safety and accounting index systems. I had discovered a package designed by a finance broker in Sydney called Finance Finder. The concept was great, but the software needed to be rewritten. I offered to use my contacts to design and build a new system based on his original design. We agreed on terms, and I stupidly agreed to him holding 51%. Harley now controlled the company. It was the worst business relationship I had ever endured. The day I accepted his pitiful offer for my share was a happy day indeed.

Harley insisted I go to Melbourne to launch the company there. I lived with my second cousin, Lois, who made life tolerable considering I was separated from my ten-year-old and eight-year- old daughters, Emma and Sophie.

After ten months with some success I told Harley I was opting out and intended to return to Brisbane.

I joined a privately owned company called Dialog. The managing director was a strange dude who tried to entice women in the office to have a relationship.

I was very successful with some very large contracts, but he changed the rules and negated my commissions. Here we go again. The only positive event was meeting my now wife of twenty-eight years, Anna.

It was my intention to sue Alan as he owed me a significant amount of money. Unfortunately the lawyer I engaged was hopeless.

SEX

Yep

Chapter 8

CENSORED SECTION.

WHAT HAPPENS IN VEGAS STAYS IN VEGAS

Chapter 9

It was at Dialog that I suffered another breakdown and was off work for four weeks. I thank Alan for his support.

It was another year before I offered my resignation. At that stage Anna and I had been living together and decided to marry.

Our plan was to replicate a Four Wedding and a Funeral and get married in either the hinterland of the Gold Coast or the Sunshine Coast. We couldn't find a suitable venue. On the drive back from the Sunshine Coast, Anna suggested we get married overseas.

On our return I rang London and Paris but unfortunately we needed more time to qualify. I then called the concierge at the Hilton and asked where in Los Vegas could we get married with some class. He responded "The Little Church of the West". I booked it immediately.

Little Church of the West

Our wedding night was at Caesar's Palace; a magnificent hotel.

We flew to New York for a two-night stay at the Algonquin Hotel, a classic hotel where I had stayed before.

From New York we flew to London and then drove to Scotland where I played a round of golf at St Andrews Old Course, shooting 92. My father had played there some years before me.

We then flew to Paris and drove through France and into Italy.

We stopped at Singapore and caught up with some old friends and then back to Brisbane.

HAVE PASSPORT WILL TRAVEL

Bali was my first overseas trip in 1978

   USA – 1st trip to USA -1980

   Los Angeles

   Atlanta

   New York

   I travelled to the USA six times over all

   Boston

   New Orleans

   Seattle

   Alaska

Canada 2007

   Great Britain 1980 three times over all

   Scotland

   France 1980 x6

   Germany 2010

   Luxemburg

   Italy x 2

   Spain

   Prague

   Monaco

   Belgium

   Greece

   Turkey

   New Zealand x6

Fiji x 2

New Caledonia

Middle East

Dubai x 3

Oman

Jordan

Israel

S E Asia

Singapore x 30

Malaysia x 30

Thailand x 25

Brunei

Hong Kong x 3

Vietnam

Cambodia

Soon after we launched Future Directions version two. This time we began an I.T. recruitment company. We worked from a serviced office and turned over $1,000,000 in our first year. This converted to $2,000,000 in today's money.

My manic phase kicked in and we purchased a magnificent reproduction terrace house on terms. Unfortunately, the bank changed its terms, and the building was no longer available to us. The owners made us pay dearly.

That together with a provisional tax bill drove us into administration. It took us five years to pay our way out of it. We succeeded and went on to bigger and better things.

The company's first placement fee was $21,000 paid by a Japanese computer company. It got us on our way. Some notable placements were with Microsoft USA where we placed senior software engineers. We also placed software engineers at Google head office.

The largest fee was for a CRM specialist in South Korea the fee was $150,000.

We established a division called CRM People; CRM was an acronym for Customer Relationship Management. Most companies adopted CRM.

We became the number one listing in most of the search engines.

I designed an application to take advantage of its popularity. Large companies could use the power of our popularity to recruit their own staff.

New software was written, and we were ready to launch when my partner pulled out. I still don't understand why.

THE APPLE ISLE

Chapter 10

Brookfield House

Cromwell Close Brookfield

Brookfield was a beautiful house in Brisbane where we lived for seven years. Neither Anna nor I could tolerate the Brisbane heat and humidity and on a particularly hot and humid day we decided to move to Tasmania.

We listed our house and sold it with a $400,000 profit in 2004. The current value is $1,800,000.

The next task on the agenda was to decide where in Tasmania we would live and to find a suitable house.

After a significant amount of research we decided on the Huon Valley.

Crabtree House circa 1840

Our search discovered Crabtree House, one of the first homesteads built in Grove in the Huon Valley. We hadn't sold our Brisbane house as yet so we had to keep our fingers crossed Crabtree House would still be available when Brookfield sold. When at last we sold Brookfield we contacted the estate agent informing him we would be returning to Grove for a final inspection. He on the other hand informed us a couple from England would be inspecting the house and quite possibly buying the property the following day. As it turned out he wasn't telling us a porky.

We had only seen the house from the outside, but we were able to view many interior images. We decided to make our best offer. It was accepted and we were now the proud owners of Crabtree House situated on three acres and riverfront with trout and platypus.

There are four houses attributed to the pioneers of Grove. The Parson family were the first apple orchardists in the Huon Valley.

Silas Parsons, one of the Huon Valley's original European settlers and the region's first apple grower, built historic Grove House in 1840.

After arriving in Tasmania with his family on 15 November 1835, only 32 years after Van Diemen's Land (now Tasmania) was founded, the government offered Silas a plot of land in Hobart Town. The land was not to his liking, so he rejected it in favour of a property in the lush Huon Valley.

It was here that the Grove Estate was born. Transported convicts, assigned to him as servants, helped clear the land on which to build a grand house and plant the Huon's first apple orchard.

He built a fine, roomy, house of split timber, with stone chimneys, lath and plaster rooms, and a big old English fireplace. In the garden he planted ornamental trees. In 1840, he planted three acres of the pioneer orchard of the Huon, trees which still bear fruit to this day. (Charles Parsons, son of Silas Parsons, October 10, 1921)

"My father landed on this island with his wife and family of two little girls on the ship, 'The Brothers', in 1835. The government offered my father a grant of land somewhere in the vicinity of McRobies Gully Hobart, but the land was not to his liking and he decided to look for a more suitable place. He finally selected and purchased lands at the entrance to the Huon Valley, where he founded the 'Grove Estate'. With the help of his assigned servants (transported convicts), he cleared the land, making periodical visits to Hobart Town to see his family." (Charles Parsons, son of Silas Parsons, October 10, 1921.)

Grove House holds many stories of a rich and colourful past. Among these are several alleged ghost sightings, and accounts of the house being used as an unofficial post office for outback settlers. Rocky Whelan, who later became an infamous bushranger, was among those who used to stop in to collect the mail.

This fine old building has remained a Huon Valley landmark for the last 180 years, and today helps to provide an enduring legacy for both the Huon Valley and Tasmania.

Crabtree House in the Beautiful Huon Valley

Crabtree River Cottages

Anna and I settled in well. We were introduced to many in the community by Di Millar who has since passed.

Anna and I decided to build two cottages on the river and let them out as short-term accommodation. We named them Eliza Cottage and Emily Cottage after the Parsons girls.

The council approved the building on the same title as Crabtree House. We operated the cottages very successfully until the Global Financial Crisis hit the world. We decided to sell the cottages as we borrowed money to build them. We were able to obtain separate title and sold them for a significant amount.

I managed and cleaned them for the new owner for an additional two years. I then handed the responsibilities over.

The Concerts
Chapter 11

I have attended many concerts over my lifetime. The first concert I attended was The Easy Beats at Festival Hall when I was twelve. Since then:

The Rolling Stones 3 times

    Led Zeppelin

    Rod Stewart

    Jose Feliciano

    Santana

    The Eagles

    Genesis

    Cat Stevens

    The Bee Gees

    Rick Wakeman

    Fleetwood Mac

    The Beach Boys

    Jethro Tull

    Powder Finger

    John Fogarty (Creedence)

    SKY

    Bob Dylan

    Fairport Convention 3 times

    T.Rex

    Dire Straits

Little River Band
The Chieftains
Pink Floyd
Joe Cocker
Paul Simon
AC/DC
Billy Thorpe
Daddy Cool

I'm sure I have forgotten a few.

PHILANTHROPY

Chapter 12

Anna and I had been living in the Huon Valley for a year when a significant event occurred.

There is a corner shop in Grove cleverly called The Grove Store. It was owned by Dave and Lucy Roberts and their son Joe and daughter Teresa.

I entered the shop one morning and sensed a feeling of sadness I asked Merle who also worked in the shop what was wrong.

'My 35-year-old niece Melanie died last night.'

'Oh that is sad.'

'What makes it worse she had five children under ten. The youngest was 18 months.'

'What about her husband?'

'He won't be able to work. He needs to look after the children.'

I left the store and drove down to Huonville to purchase some groceries at Woolworths. I then decided to pop into my favourite coffee shop. I began to think what I could do to help the family. I had an idea. I returned to the store and spoke to Dave.

'Dave, I would like to establish a trust to raise money to support the family.'

Dave thought it was a great idea and suggested we run the idea by Rosie Baker, the local solicitor.

Rosie and her husband Roger, a lawyer, agreed to support the concept. Both knew Melanie since she was a baby.

The next step was to get approval from John and Carol Brown, Melanie's parents.

Within a week a trust was established.

The trust comprised of:

Me

Dave Roberts

John Brown

Clinton Brown (Melanie's brother)

Rosie Baker

I contacted the Mercury newspaper they agreed to publish a full-page story.

Channel 9 contacted me and asked if A Current Affair could run a story. We raised $60,000 from that exposure.

Sunrise Channel 7 also contacted me and ran a story. The four-person crew stayed at Crabtree House.

I organised a concert at a local vineyard, Home Hill. A newsreader, Jo Palmer who is now an MP hosted it.

We had several bands and an auction, which raised $20,000.

We had five television programs and four newspaper articles and a double page in Take Five.

We raised $140,000.

Joe Roberts, Dave Roberts and Rosie Baker have since died.

I was yet again in the Grove Store when Joe Roberts passed me an A4 type written sheet. A family was asking for help as their ten-year-old daughter, Jessie, was dying from cancer. She had asked her parents take her to Fiji as a last request. They couldn't afford it.

I took it on. I contacted several resorts and finally four agreed to accommodate the family for a week each. All expenses were covered.

Treasure Island. One of the Resorts

They had a great time. Jessie's mother put a holiday album for me, which I appreciated.

Jessie died three months later. Her parents separated soon after.

LET THEM RIP

I read a News Limited article some time ago re some of the 18,000 Australian soldiers from WW1 being ploughed back into the fields in northern France by French farmers based on Paul Daley's and Mike Bower's experience in Northern France.

The Department of Veteran Affairs and the Department of Defence did not believe this was happening and believed it was all media spin. The response to my email to Warren Snowdon, Minister for Veteran Affairs, and the Prime Minister answering Andrew Wilkie's question in Parliament certainly reflect this view.

Paul and Mike's French guide was a man called Dominique who has lived in Northern France for many years and has the utmost respect for our diggers. He has witnessed and reported to the Commonwealth War Graves Commission many occurrences of soldiers' remains being covered over once they have been revealed because to report them is a long and protracted procedure which delays their farming and excavating unduly.

My intent was to encourage the Australian Government to invest in establishing The Missing Diggers Institute to ensure our soldiers are to rest in peace after being killed in such a horrific way.

The Institute could be a subsidiary organisation of the CWGC

I am astounded that the majority of our politicians, business leaders and media professionals have chosen to completely ignore my request for an investigation into our missing diggers. They are there on

Remembrance Day and ANZAC Day and repeat the words "Lest We Forget" yet it seems they have forgotten.

Even if there is only a slight chance that our diggers are being treated so badly, they should act.

I have spoken to eyewitnesses living near the various battlefields and they assure me this is happening every year.

Julia Gillard automated response
Kevin Rudd (Department responded on his behalf)
Warren Snowden (Responded see Ministers Response)
Tony Abbott automated response
Andrew Wilkie (Asked the Prime Minister a Question in Parliament see Gillard's Response)
Bob Katter Contacted twice, twice ignored
Tony Windsor Ignored
Rob Oakshot Ignored
Bob Brown (Thank you for sharing from a staff member)
Malcolm Turnbull (Responded and has acted but no real action)
Stewart Robert (responded, accepts Warren Snowdon's explanation without any investigation)
DVA (have responded but denied it is happening)
Dick Smith No Response
Geoff Cousins (responded but declined to help)
Kerry Stokes (referred to Corporate Affairs who referred me to the Australian War Museum)
Alan Jones (approached twice; twice ignored)
Ray Hadley (approached twice; twice ignored)
All TV stations
RSLs in each state (two have acknowledged. Tasmania has supported)

Questioner Mr WILKIE
Responder Ms GILLARD
Speaker Question No.
War Graves
Mr WILKIE (Denison) (14:3 9):
My question is to the Prime Minister. The remains of World War I diggers are often uncovered during routine earthworks on farms and

building sites in France and Belgium. There have been concerning reports that these remains are sometimes ploughed back into the ground or simply ignored when they are uncovered. I understand the government's position is that this practice does not occur and it would cite Fromelles as an exemplar of what does occur when remains are found. Given the numerous reports documenting this occurrence, will the government look afresh at this issue and work with the French and Belgian governments to give greater protection to the remains of our World War I diggers?

Ms GILLARD (Labor—Prime Minister) (14:3 9):
I thank the member for Denison for his question. It is a very serious one and I am sure all members of the parliament will have an interest in the answer. We are all committed in this parliament, this government, all Australian governments, to remembering and honouring our war dead. It is one of the things that has bound us together as a nation over a very long period of time. It is part of the contract between our nation and those who have served for us in battle. It is a commitment that I take very seriously.
The treaties that Australia and the Commonwealth have with France relating to our war dead are amongst the strongest treaties of their kind. French and Belgian officials and those who own and farm the land in which remains are sometimes found understand the desire of Australians to ensure that any remains are dealt with sensitively and they share our concern about treating our war dead with respect.
I am advised that there is no evidence that French farmers are guilty of ploughing human remains back into their fields, as has sometimes been asserted in media reporting. In recent years most if not all remains of Australian soldiers have been discovered at a depth greater than that which is uncovered by routine ploughing. They are further underground. In almost every instance those remains were discovered during deeper excavations—for example, when people are digging trenches for gas pipelines, so they are working further underground.
As all Australians know, tens of thousands of Australians fell in battle across the Western Front. There are about 18,000 Australians who lost their lives and for whom there is no known grave. The government will continue to do all it can to find and identify the remains of our war dead. The member for Denison referred to Fromelles, for example. We

continue to identify and commemorate the remains of 250 soldiers. Those remains were discovered in 2009.

The government has set up a new unit known as the Unrecovered War Casualties section to specifically investigate missing-in-action cases.

Finally, I want to recognise—and I think members of the House would join me in this—the respect and gratitude and constant acts of remembrance that the people of France and Belgium pay to Australia. People who have visited there comment on it, not only in terms of the memorials they see but also in the attitudes of the people they meet. We continue to be grateful for seeing that emotion from the people of France and the people in Belgium towards our soldiers lost at war.

(Denison) (NaN.NaN pm)

(Lalor) (NaN.NaN pm)

I sent Julia a video of seven dead at ground level.

SACRED SOIL

The next project I undertook was Sacred Soil.

Project Management Plan and Overview

Sacred Soil was a project to collect soil from the battlefields and war cemeteries where Australian Diggers fought and died and are buried at Gallipoli and the Western Front, and to return this soil to Australia and create a Memorial/Sacred Garden in each Capital City. As stated the proposal was originally conceived as a national project, however apart from limited interest by South Australia no other state responded with interest or commitment to the project. Initial contact was made to each of the State Presidents of the RSL. Despite this seemingly lack of initial interest, the development team decided to push ahead with the concept and to make this project unique to the lasting memory of Tasmanians who participated in this momentous event in our history.

More and more young people are remembering, honouring and participating in the numerous government-sponsored educational competitions to win and participate in two-week study tours to significant areas at Gallipoli and/or the Western Front. Although World War 1 took place one hundred years ago, young Australians are giving truth to the words "Lest We Forget" and our plan is to incorporate the collection of the soil as part of their study tour. We envisage that the inclusion of this activity into their battlefield pilgrimages will give them a greater understanding of the sacrifices made by all who participated. Unfortunately the fields of battle in Africa and the Middle East cannot be included due to the extremely high risk factor in today's political environment.

This project is one that we believe encapsulates the true spirit of ANZAC and one which will offer families who cannot, through various means travel to the Battlefields to visit sites where relatives who made the ultimate sacrifice died, a symbolic garden to visit and to reflect and honour the fallen. We propose that a series of plaques be erected on each site identifying the battlefield collection point and more significantly thanking the Governments of the Republic of France and Belgium for their significant contribution and cooperation.

Stakeholder Roles and Responsibilities
Key Stake Holders

Garry Willmott – Project founder

Robert Dick – Project Manager

Alex Dick –IT/Legal adviser

RSL Tasmania

Department of Education - Tasmania

Department of Veteran Affairs ensured Sacred Soil would not happen. Why? I don't know.

Queen of Hearts Foundation

When Princess Diana tragically died there was an outpouring of grief around the world. A significant amount of money was donated to charities which Dianna supported. The issue I saw was a significant amount was being donated from Australian and other countries to English charities. I established Queen of Hearts with the purpose of ensuring Australian donations would be funnelled to Australian charities in Diana's name.

I established contact the Diana Trust. Richard Branson through his PA PWC and various other organisations who were involved.

We developed a website and my good friend Cenred and I wrote a song. Several newspaper articles were written and I was interviewed on ABC radio.

Just as we received approval it was suddenly withdrawn due to tax law between England and Australia prohibiting it.

COVID

During the middle of the COVID pandemic the Federal Government provided grants to the tourism industry to all states except Tasmania.

I contacted Andrew Wilkie suggesting that Tasmania was suffering a chronic lack of visitors from the other states and therefore our tourism industry was suffering.

He agreed and contacted the PM.

Andrew suggested I also contact Julie Collins. I spoke with her and she too agreed Tasmania deserved grants. She raised the subject twice in Federal Parliament.

A grant of $7000 was allocated to each tourism operator.

Both Andrew and Julie reported back to me.

HIT THE ROAD JACK

Crabtree Road was in a terrible state potholes and significant cracks in the bitumen along the length of the so-called sealed road. The road had become a dangerous carriageway.

I decided to speak to the Mayor of Huonville, but he dismissed my suggestion to reseal the road. It all came down to funding.

My next step was to establish a petition. I was able to accumulate 100 signatures, but the council remained steadfast. I raised another petition three months later. It worked; Crabtree Road is now a smooth, well-cared-for road.

PAPERBACK WRITER

Chapter 13

It was a news article about our soldiers being reburied in the fields of France and Belgium that raised my interest. Paul Daley, a Canberra based author and journalist, wrote the original article based on his experience. I contacted Paul and registered my interest and enquired how I could help. An online paper contacted me and requested I write an article about the reburied diggers. I agreed and it was very well received. I approached Paul with the idea he write a book using a story line I had developed.

Paul liked the concept but suggested I write the book as he had other projects in the pipeline.

I responded with, 'I can't write a book.'

'Of cause you can.'

So I did; I began writing *The Other Side of the Trench*.

I began to receive very positive reviews including one from Eric Bogel, one of Australia's greatest songwriters.

Hello Garry

Sorry about delay in replying, but the shadows of the festive season descended early on me, and left late.... it's only in the last week or so I've had the time to sit down with a glass or two of red and read a few books, including yours......a personal and moving account Garry, I've read quite a few similar books in my time, all telling deeply personal accounts of courage and tragedy, real stories about real human beings in unimaginably horrific situations, and yours ranks with the best of them. I wonder if many of those WWI generals slept all that soundly after the war was over...

Kind regards
Eric Bogle
Writer of "The Band Played Waltzing Matilda" & "Green Hills of France"

THE OTHER SIDE OF THE TRENCH

Garry,
Your research, your narrative has immersed me in a world hitherto unknown to me.
The accounts you've given have made the suffering of our soldiers so immediate, so graphic that one cannot help but be deeply moved…and of course, angry at the current neglect of politicians and others, apathetic about their remains. This will be an important book, which will engage readers in the reality of suffering, both physical and spiritual, not only of the soldiers but also of their families.
It's a story that needs to be told.
I hope I have helped by editing it as carefully as it deserves.
Best Wishes
Janet Upcher

This Review was in the Daily Telegraph on April 22, 2014
The Other Side Of The Trench Garry Willmott Port Campbell Press, $27
In his books The Other Side Of The Trench and Brothers In Arms Garry Willmott cleverly blends fact with fiction to transport the reader

beyond the tragedy of the Great War and into the spirits of the men who fought it. Willmott's books are well researched and cunningly composed, using photographs from the front, newspaper cuttings and historical accounts to create a solid foundation for the bursts of fiction where the imagination of a man who lost two great-uncles and a grandfather in World War I can run wild. Willmott is driven by a personal mission to find the remains of his great-uncles Harry junior and Harry senior, among the estimated 18,000 Australians who died on the Western Front but have no known grave.
Ian McPhedran NEWS LTD

Ian McPhedran is the Sydney based national defence writer for News Limited. He has been a journalist all his working life and has covered conflicts in Burma, Somalia, Cambodia, Papua New Guinea, Indonesia, East Timor, Afghanistan and Iraq. In 1993 he won a United Nations Association peace media award and in 1999 the Walkley award for best news report for his expose of the navy's Collins class submarine fiasco. His first book, The Amazing SAS: the inside story of Australia's special forces, is a national best seller. McPhedran lives in Balmain with his wife Verona and daughter Lucy.

I enjoyed writing and continued on. I have now written, including this autobiography, 24 books.
Some other reviews.

BROTHERS IN ARMS

Excellent book. It reads like a murder mystery (which it actually is). I really enjoyed it and couldn't put it down once I got started!!! You are to be highly commended.
Dave Crooks
USA

Not my usual type, but enjoyed every word. It was a real page-turner. Kept my attention from start to the end.
Mrs Kimberley D Krarup

Brothers in Arms was not only a compelling read I learned so much about the horrific wars of the 20th century. I highly recommend it.
A.L. Shearer

ESCAPE

4.0 out of 5 stars
Much Better Than I Expected.
I have always have been a fan of "military escape stories". Having read quite many, I did not expect much from the book. Much to my surprise, it contained stories that I had not read before. Volume contains stories from many conflicts. If you are an "adventure" fan, this volume is good.

5.0 out of 5 stars
True Heroes we need to Honor, November 29, 2013
Amazon Verified Purchase (What's this?)

ESCAPE - TRUE ACCOUNTS OF POW ESCAPES (KINDLE EDITION)

Truth is stranger than fiction in regards to these stories. It is amazing that so many men could communicate in a foreign land and not be caught. I could not believe the terrible treatment that the Japanese gave their captives. I am going to have my son read this!

RED LIGHTS ON THE SOMME

This book is one of the best books I have ever read. When I finished reading it I felt like I wanted to read it again. I highly recommend it.
Von Gracey
Co - Founder, Pozieres Remembrance Association

THE OTHER SIDE OF THE TRENCH

I've just sat up this evening to finish your incredible book.

I'm extremely, extremely sorry at the late reply and the delay of finishing your novel - however it's been very busy with current year 12 studies/commitments, and having to read the drab books they select for us at school.

However, I was deeply moved by your novel.

The personal connection I was able to make with each one of the diggers within the story - due to the family members participating on the tour within the book, was something very special, and each one of their stories were extraordinary.

Having been to visit many of the sites within your novel, also made this book very interesting for me, and I learnt many new things about different conflicts in areas that I had not known about prior to reading your book.

The photographs throughout the book, I believe, gave it a very personal feeling, and was once again a very clear reminder that this is not just a made up story - that these were real men, and that it was a real war, though it is hard to even imagine what it was like for these men.

I am extremely interested in your 'Let Them Rip' program, and your epilogue at the end of the novel was very powerful, and hit home for me.

I am passing on your book for my mother to read - as she has a very deep interest in war history, having had her grandfather - my great-grandfather - fight on the Western Front at Bullecourte and Pozieres in WWI. I will let you know what she thinks, I'm sure she will feel the same way as me.

I am more than positive that each of the prizewinners would be honoured to receive one of your books - as I was - and I know that it will be a treasure for myself, that I will pass down the story to hopefully in the future my own children.

The work you are doing is incredible Garry. I know it is very difficult for you to get the Government moving, however if your program helps even one of these soldiers rest in peace, then I believe it is completely worthwhile. What you are doing is monumental, and very admirable.

I hope to stay in contact with you in the future, and I am going to look into what I am able to do in my local community, and further on in my life, in regards to your program, and others similar.

All the best, and once again thank-you for giving me the opportunity to read your book, it was truly my honour and pleasure.

Kindest Regards,
Jasmine
College Captain - Sacred Heart College Geelong

RED LIGHTS ON THE SOMME

I thoroughly enjoyed 'Red Lights on the Somme' not a wasted word was to be found - This book is written in a striking style and has great force in its realism and delivery. One of my lasting impressions from this book is its representation of the fickleness of war, of life, for all those lads. A great book - VERY readable. Thank you Garry Wilmott - I am coming back for more.

Guy Walton - Singer Songwriter

A BOOK THAT I COULD NOT PUT DOWN.
I have just completed reading another book by Garry Willmott; "Red Lights on the Somme". Garry's compelling reading of our diggers on the Western Front was more than I expected having read many books on the Western Front. While reading this book I was in the moment alongside these men. What a fantastic read and what made it better for me was while reading this amazing book I was on the Western Front at the time. This book is a must read. Well done Garry and I will be reading more of your books soon. Thank you for the dedication and the research that you put into your books. I have 3 Great-Uncles who fought on the Western Front only 1 has a grave. Thank you for remembering them in a style that makes it fun to read but also you learn something on every page.

Kind regards
Yvonne Hall
Coffs Harbour

Colour Blind - Bullets and Shells Don't Discriminate

Educating and entertaining are the two words I would use to describe the latest book Colour Blind by GS Willmott. Mr Willmott has the knack to deliver interesting information about the battles of World War I as well as getting you involved in the human side of it. I enjoyed travelling on the journeys of our diggers and learning just how difficult it was for the indigenous people of Australia to not just fight but to enlist to fight for our country and get the recognition for their efforts that they so rightly deserved.
Kim

You Forgot the Sauce

"You Forgot the Sauce" written by Mr G. Willmott was one of the best books I have read over the summer break. It goes at a break neck pace with twists and turns at every corner. I am suitably impressed at Garry's literary abilities and look forward to a sequel.
Tony Pittard
Company Director
Melbourne

SMALL FARM WARRIORS

For those with an interest in Australian Military History, this book not only draws one's interest to the life in the trenches of WW1 and to their sons in WW2 that occurred twenty years later, but also 'larrikinism' of the Aussie digger abroad during these periods in history.
This book held my interest for its full length with just the right amount of all the emotions depicted. The ups and downs of the men both when serving and on their return to Australia.
A well-researched and written book, which does not disguise the author's interest in the Soldier Settlers of Australia and Commonwealth countries. Definitely a good read and I do hope it gets published.

All in all a bloody good read and well worth your effort. We have been honoured and privileged to assist, hope we have helped in some way.
Regards
Faye & Geoff Threlfall

YOU FORGOT THE SAUCE

You Forgot the Sauce' is a poignant, contemporaneous story. A well-researched, and easy read.
Lysbeth Driesen

CAUGHT BETWEEN TWO WORLDS

Garry's story-based historical plight of Vietnam in its bid to release itself from the shackles of colonialism cleverly intertwines factual and fictional in a fast-paced, gripping and easy to read the story. While a few facets of the war are retold in great detail the book focuses on the exciting personal story of an Aussie soldier and a Vietnamese girl during the conflict. The story continues post-conflict, with the couple running a successful global business and with the help of military friends and serious weaponry destroy a murderous, drug trafficking ring.
The writer obviously knows the history of this part of the world and has woven a thread of intrigue and mayhem throughout the book up to the very last paragraph. Very well written, highly enjoyable and a book that can be read in one sitting.
I look forward to Garry's next book and hope it will be as good as this one.
Martin Humphries

Many congratulations on a most moving but exciting book.
I remembered where I left off after she was enlisted in the Vietcong.
A very sad story of a wonderful family who despite the odds become so successful.
Well written & hard to put down as I became so interested as to what was next.
I hope you do very well with sales.
David

THE FAB SIXTIES

The Sixties, what a decade. So many events that changed the world, for better or worse.
This book written by Garry Willmott takes us on a journey of discovery, through the sixties, encompassing assassinations, the space race, presidents, good and bad, wars, The Cuba Crisis, many major music festivals, and many other earth-shattering events.
This book written by Garry Willmott takes us on a journey of discovery, through the sixties, encompassing assassinations, the space race, presidents, good and bad, wars, The Cuba Crisis, many major music festivals, and many other earth-shattering events.
Garry has written this with passion, with fervour, and with absolute knowledge of his subject matter. His research is beyond good, it is excellent. His technique and overall skill in taking us on a journey and making us feel a part of it all shows a skill not many authors possess.
I heartily recommend this book to anyone interested in history, the facts both real and sometimes unnerving, and anyone up for a really sensational read. I believe this book is brilliant and needs to be read by all.
Ian Jones

Hi Garry, loved your book "The Fab 60's." It instantly transported me back in time. It was either instant recall of events and sometimes, "I had forgotten that".
Dawn Potocnik

In a delightful romp down memory lane, funny, factual and fast Garry has brought back many memories good and bad from the 'roaring 60's'. Garry's style of mixing fact with some fiction makes it incredibly easy to read, cover to cover in one sitting.
A great read for anyone that was there even if you can remember it.
Martin Humphries

GRAND DECEPTIONS

Grand Deceptions is a wonderful read. Its interconnecting familial stories were full of intrigue and cleverly balanced with interesting encounters holding my interest to the very end. Well-done Garry!
Your history references were quite extraordinary and well sequenced throughout the story. Trish

5.0 out of 5 stars Probably the author's most comprehensive effort to date
Reviewed in the United States on 10 May 2023
Verified Purchase
Very absorbing, with the author's usual outstanding research and a comprehensive plot built around real-life events. The author manages to keep his storyline at his usual rapid pace while building a deep profile of the time and the people. I found it not only absorbing, but also providing facts that were new to me (who knew there could be up to 150 riders turning up for a fox hut)?
Overall an enjoyable read from this prolific writer and I would recommend it to anyone who enjoys historical fiction. Good stuff.

BOY'S OWN WAR

Finished your book and its pure brilliant literature, great research. Recommended. If you don't mind I'll pass it on to a mate of mine. Must purchase your Somme book soon. Good health. wish ISIS would take a leaf out of it
If you have even a slight interest in war or history the causes and effects this book is for you. Short concise stories that will have you wanting more. Hard to believe it's fiction, it's that good. 10/10

Boy's Own War is a brilliant piece of literature based on sound research. If you have even a slight interest in military history this book will capture your imagination. Willmott's stories will have you wanting more; I give it a rating of five stars.

THE LAST PIRATE HANGED

Garry has developed into the master of his genre. A very tall man among us mere mortals. A sincere and robust storyteller who deserves every tribute. This work is his best yet.
Andy Causon artist and friend

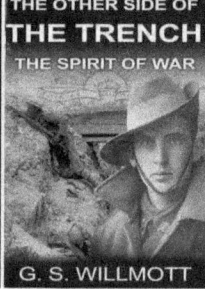

OPERATION GARRY

Chapter 14

I thought a little light medical history could be interesting.

Tonsils age 4

Appendix age 16

Anal Fissure age 35

Brain Tumour age 38

Varicose Veins age 42

Gall Bladder age 44

Pace Maker age 56

I have had various visits to hospital.

Pneumonia X 6

Influenza A

Stroke

It's amazing I'm still alive.

FAMILY TREASURES

Chapter 15

There are a few treasures that will stay in the family; I will list them by age.

Antique Indian Ebony Box

My grandmother gave this ebony box to my father after he had admired it as a boy.

Her grandfather was a tailor in London. He was commissioned by a lord to tailor two suits. When he returned to collect the suits he apologised, explaining he had recently lost his fortune. He asked my ancestor if he would accept this Indian ebony box. He agreed. It has been in our family ever since.

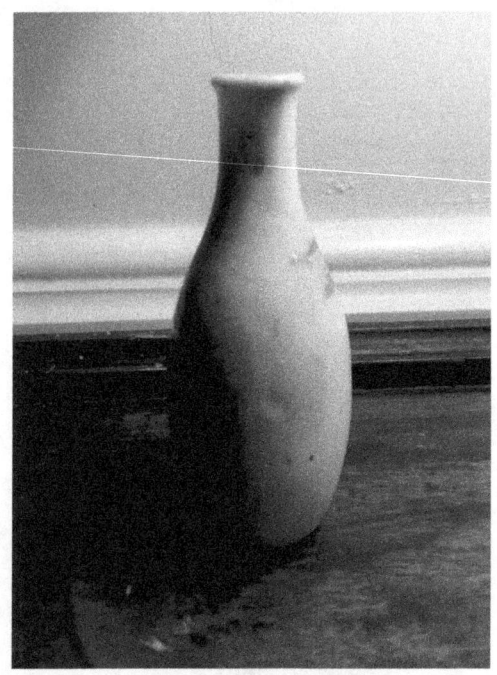

Saki Jar Hiroshima

My dad is on the far right

My father was 1st Officer on a merchant ship called The Duntroon during WW2 and after.

The Duntroon brought the first troops into Hiroshima three months after the atomic bomb.

He found this sake jar amongst the rubble. It was the only thing he or his other officers found.
The photo above displays the jar on the Hiroshima waterfront.

My father's biological mother died when my dad was very young. He told me he remembered sitting in the gutter crying as the black horses took his mother's hearse away.

She left him a gold brooch which he later got made into a pair of cufflinks and a signet ring. When my father died he left this jewellery to me. The photo above is of the ring which I wear constantly.

Family History

Chapter 16

Two significant events happened in my family history.

Samuel Willmott was born in Woods Point. He moved to Melbourne and became the city's first auctioneer. He accumulated significant wealth and constructed the Bee Hive Building incorporating the Block Arcade in 1891. Both are still standing and regarded as classical architecture.

Samuel was my great-grandfather.

Main Street Woods Point

Woods Point Hotel. One of 36 during the gold rush

Woods point featured heavily in the Willmott history. I have highlighted it in red.

The Beehive Building

The Block Arcade

The second significant event was when the three Willmott brothers, Edward, Samuel and my grandfather, William, embarked on a cattle drive from Woods Point, Victoria to Western Australia. It took three years and was fraught with danger.

Once they arrived my grandfather, the youngest of the three brothers, broke his leg while mustering. Once the leg had healed he announced to his two older brothers that he intended to return to Melbourne. They gave him his ship fare back but nothing from the cattle sales or his three years' wages. That was the end of the brotherly relationship.

EDWARD WILLMOTT **was born Abt.** *1740* **in Luton Bedfordshire. He married** SARAH HAWKINS. **She was born** *1744. History of Luton https://en.wikipedia.org/wiki/Luton*

Children *of* EDWARD WILLMOTT and SARAH HAWKINS are:

1. ELIZABETH WILLMOTT, b. Abt. 1769, Hertfordshire, Bedford.

2. SAMUEL WILLMOTT *(EDWARD1)* was born Abt. *1770* in Kimpton Hertfordshire England. **Married** ANN WELCH

3. MARTHA WILLMOTT, b. Abt. 1775, Hertfordshire, Bedford.

2. SAMUEL WILLMOTT *(EDWARD1)* **was born Abt.** *1770* **in Kimpton Hertfordshire England. He married** ANN WELCH *21 Nov 1795* **in Kimpton Hertfordshire England'. She was born Abt.** *1775* **in Hertfordshire England.**

Children of SAMUEL WILLMOTT and ANN WELCH are:

2.1 SAMUEL WILLMOTT, b. 27 Dec 1801, Kimpton Hertfordshire. **Married** ELIZABETH YOUNG 1841 Samuel Barleybins farm Kimpton near Ivorys 1851 Elizabeth is a widow at Mackerie End Farm with children.

2.2 JOHN WILLMOTT was born 02 Oct 1809 in Kimpton, Hertfordshire. **Married** MARY LAWMAN

2.3 MARTHA WILLMOTT *(SAMUEL(2), EDWARD(1))* was born *17 March 1805* in Kimpton

Hertfordshire. **Married** FREDERICK SWAIN THEN A JAMES PARROTT

2.4   ELIZABETH WILLMOTT was born 30 Mar 1800 in Kimpton Hertfordshire. **Married** JOSEPH SCOTT

2.5   EDWARD WILLMOTT, b. 10 Apr 1796, Kimpton Hertfordshire. **Married** RACHEL ?

2.6   MARY WILLMOTT was born 05 Jun 1808 in Kimpton Hertfordshire. **Married** DANIEL CREW

2.7   CHARLOTTE WILLMOTT was born 12 Jun 1803 in Kimpton Hertfordshire. **Married** WILLIAM LINES

2.8   HENRY WILLMOTT *(SAMUEL (2), EDWARD(1))* was born *07* Sep *1806* in Kimpton Hertfordshire. **Married** ESTER ELIZABETH ? THEN A LOUISA BROWN.

2.9   SARAH WILLMOTT, b. 16 Sep 1798, Kimpton Hertfordshire.

2.10   JOSEPH WILLMOTT *(SAMUEL (2), EDWARD(1))* was born 24 Nov 1811 in Kimpton Hertfordshire. **Married** MARY ? AND A EMMA ?

Census information: A William Willmott is miller, Ippolites Mill Pigots 1839 brother Henry Willmott and William Willmott farmers Harpenden 1851 Note Ann poss. Welch is mother of Will Lines so Charlotte and Will poss. first cousins? 1841 census Wheathampstead, William Lines 46 Smith, Charlotte W 38, Catherine D 14, Henry S 12, John S 10, Ann D 8, Clementine D 4, Edward S 3 Albert S 1. 1851 Census Wheathamsptead, William Lines 56, Smith, born Luton BFD, Charlotte Lines W 47 born Kings Walden, Henry Lines S 22 Smith Wheathamsptead, John Lines S 20 Smith Whstd, Ann D 18 Bonnetsewer, Whstd, William S 16 Apprentice Whstd, Clementine D 14 Scholar, Edward S 12 Whstd, Albert Lines S 11 Whstd, Elizabeth D 9 Whstd, Mry Lines D 7 Whstd. 1861 census Kimpton William 66 farmer 110 acres 2 men, 2 boys, William Lines buried Kimpton Parish Church age 69 death April 19 1864 with wife Charlotte, age 71, died Oct 28 1875

2.1. SAMUEL WILLMOTT, b. 27 Dec 1801, Kimpton Hertfordshire. **He married** ELIZABETH YOUNG *04* Jan *1827* **in Shenley Hertfordshire England, daughter** *of* DANIEL YOUNG and MARY. **She was born 11 Sep** *1803* **in Kings Walden Hertfordshire England.** Samuel was recorded as a brewer.

Children of SAMUEL WILLMOTT and ELIZABETH YOUNG are:

2.1.1   SAMUEL CHARLES WILLMOTT, b. Abt. Apr 1837, Kings Walden Hertfordshire; d. 04 Nov 1894,

Woods Point Victoria.

2.1.2   CHARLES WILLMOTT, b. Abt. Nov 1828, Kings Walden Hertfordshire England. **Married** EMMA ? B. 1821

Married in 1851 in Holly Bush Hall.

2.1.3   ELIZABETH WILLMOTT, b. Abt. Apr 1831,,Bendish Kings Walden Hertfordshire England. **Married** ISSAC ARNOLD

2.1.4   MARY WILLMOTT, b. Abt. Jun 1832, Kings Walden Hertfordshire England.

2.1.5   CHARLOTTE WILLMOTT, b. Abt. Apr 1834, Frogmore Kings Walden Hertfordshire England.

2.1.6   EDWARD WILLMOTT, b. Abt. Mar 1839, Barley Beans Kimpton Hertfordshire.

2.1.7   ANN WILLMOTT, b. Abt. Apr 1841, Barley Beans Kimpton Hertfordshire.

2.1.8   EMMA WILLMOTT, b. Abt. Jan 1844, Wheathampstead Hertfordshire.

2.1.9   ELLENA WILLMOTT, b. Abt. May 1845, Wheathampstead Hertfordshire.

2.2   JOHN WILLMOTT **was born**.02 Oct 1809 **in Kimpton Hertfordshire. He married** MARY LAWMAN.

Children of JOHN WILLMOTT and MARY LAWMAN are:

2.2.1   SAMUEL WILLMOTT, b 6 Nov 1853 in Royston Hertfordshire. History of Royston https://en.wikipedia.org/wiki/Royston,_Hertfordshire

2.3   MARTHA WILLMOTT *(SAMUEL(2), EDWARD(1))* **was born** *17 March 1805* **in Kimpton**

Hertfordshire. She married FREDERICK SWAIN *08 MARCH 1837* **in Kimpton Hertfordshire England.**

She then remarried a JAMES PARROTT

Children of MARTHA WILLMOTT and FREDERICK SWAIN are:

2.3.1   WILLIAM SWAIN, b. Abt March 1839, Peters Green England

2.4   ELIZABETH WILLMOTT **was born** 30 Mar 1800 **in Kimpton Hertfordshire. She Married** JOSEPH SCOTT

2.5   EDWARD WILLMOTT **was born** 10 Apr 1796, **Kimpton Hertfordshire**. He Married Rachel in Hertfordshire England.

Children of EDWARD WILLMOTT and RACHEL are:

2.5.1   ANN WILLMOTT b. 1817– christened in Kings Walden History of Kings Walden https://en.wikipedia.org/wiki/King%27s_Walden

2.5.2   FRANCES WILLMOTT b. 1825 – christened in Kings Walden

2.5.3   MELISSA WILLMOTT b. 1819– christened in St Ippolits

2.5.4   JOHN WILLMOTT b. 1821 – christened in St Ippolits

2.5.5   CHARLES WILLMOTT b. 1828 – Hertfordshire

2.5.6   AMELIA WILLMOTT b. 1823 Hertfordshire d. 1900. **married** THOMAS IVORY GATWARD b. 1824 Peters Green

Hertfordshire d. 1903 Luton, married in 1845

2.6   MARY WILLMOTT **was born** 05 Jun 1808 **in Kimpton Hertfordshire. She married** DANIEL CREW 14 Jun 1836 **in Kimpton Hertfordshire England.** Daniel was born 14 Aug 1808 (baptised) in Kings Walden. He married Hannah Joiner and had 3 children. He then married Mary.

Children of MARY WILLMOTT and DANIEL CREW are:

2.6.1   HENRY CREW, b.1837 Kimpton Hertfordshire. Baptism 18 March 1839 History of Kimpton https://en.wikipedia.org/wiki/Kimpton,_Hertfordshire
2.6.2   EDMUND CREW, b 1837 Kimpton Hertfordshire, Baptism 18 March 1839 – Died: 1864
2.6.3   ALFRED CREW, b. 1842 Kimpton Hertfordshire, Baptism 3 Feb 1842 – Died: 1849
2.6.4   MARY CREW, b.1846 Kimpton Hertfordshire, Baptism 27 Sept 1846

2.7 CHARLOTTE WILLMOTT **was born** 12 Jun 1803 **in Kimpton Hertfordshire. She married** WILLIAM LINES 27 April 1826 **in Kings Walden Hertfordshire.**

Children of CHARLOTTE WILLMOTT and WILLIAM LINES

2.7.1 CATHERINE LINES b. 1828 Wheathamstead. History of Wheathamstead https://en.wikipedia.org/wiki/Wheathampstead

2.7.2 HENRY LINES, b 1829 Wheathamstead

2.7.3 JOHN LINES b, 1830 Wheathamstead

2.7.4 ANN LINES b, 1833 Wheathamstead. **Married** Jonas Hawkes

2.7.5 WILLIAM LINES b, 1834 Wheathamstead

2.7.6 CLEMENTINA LINES b, 1837 Wheathamstead

2.7.7 EDWARD LINES b, 1838 Wheathamstead

2.7.8 ALBERT LINES b, 1840 Wheathamstead

2.7.9 ELIZABETH LINES b, 1843 Wheathamstead

2.7.10 MARY LINES b, 1845 Wheathamstead. **Married** Alfred Tomlin

2.8 HENRY WILLMOTT (SAMUEL2, EDWARD1) was born 07 Sep 1806 in Kimpton Hertfordshire. He married (1) ESTER ELIZABETH ? He then married (2) LOUISA BROWN 11 Sep 1829 **in St Albans Hertfordshire**, daughter of WILLIAM BROWN and ELIZABETH BALLARD. She was born Abt. 1807 **in Kings Walden Hertfordshire England.** Henry was recorded as a Farmer in 1861 (familysearch.org)

Children of HENRY WILLMOTT and LOUISA BROWN are:

2.8.1 JOSEPH WILLMOTT, b. Abt. 1830, Kings Walden Hertfordshire England. Married twice (refer to 2.8.1.1)

2.8.2 ELIZABETH ANN WILLMOTT, b. Abt. 1837, Sandridge, Hertfordshire. Married (refer to 2.8.2.1)

2.8.3 LOUISA WILLMOTT, b. Abt. 1839, Sandridge, Hertfordshire.

2.8.4 MARY WILLMOTT, b. Abt. 1842, Sandridge, Hertfordshire.

2.8.5   FREDERICK WILLMOTT, b. 18 Nov 1844, Harpenden Hertfordshire. (1881 census) Married (refer to 2.8.5.1)

2.8.6   SARAH MARIA WILLMOTT, b. Abt. 1846, Harpenden Hertfordshire.

2.8.7   CHARLOTTE WILLMOTT, b. Abt. 1848, Harpenden Hertfordshire.

2.8.8. JANE WILLMOTT, b. Abt. 1850, Harpenden Hertfordshire.

2.8.9. HENRY WILLMOTT, b. Abt. 1832, Kings Walden Hertfordshire England. Married (refer to 2.8.9.1)

2.8.10 SARAH WILLMOTT, b. Abt. 1840, Hertfordshire England.

2.8.11 WILLIAM WILLMOTT, b. Abt. 1838, Hertfordshire England.

2.10   JOSEPH WILLMOTT *(SAMUEL(2), EDWARD(1))* **was born** 24 Nov 1811 in **Kimpton Hertfordshire. He firstly married** MARY UNKNOWN SURNAME. **He then married** EMMA. She was born Abt. 1815 in Middlesex London.

Children of JOSEPH WILLMOTT and MARY are:

2.10.1   MARY WILLMOTT, b. Abt. 1838, Kings Walden Hertfordshire England.

2.10.2   SARAH WILLMOTT, b. Abt. 1842, Kings Walden Hertfordshire England.

2.10.3   MARY WILLMOTT (TWIN), b Abt 1839 Kings Walden Hertfordshire England

2.10.4   ANN WILLMOTT (TWIN), b Abt 1839 Kings Walden Hertfordshire England

2.1.3   ELIZABETH WILLMOTT, b. Abt. Apr 1831,Bendish Kings Walden Hertfordshire England. **Married** ISSAC ARNOLD

b. 1827 in Kings Walden Heath Hertfordshire. 1871 Farmer of 57 acres, with wife Eliz nee Willmott baby Ada and m-in-law Eliz Willmott. Brother's widow Mary and 5 children next door Coleman Green Meadows as landowner/ brewers/farmers

Children of ELIZABETH WILLMOTT and ISSAC are:

2.1.3.1   ADA ARNOLD b. 1869 Breechwood Green Kings Walden

2.5.1 ANN WILLMOTT – christened in Kings Walden married RICHARD CHRISTOPHER SWAIN on 18th April 1841 in Kimpton Hertfordshire.

2.5.4 JOHN WILLMOTT - **married** JANE CHAPMAN b. 1823 from Luton unknown date.

2.5.5 CHARLES WILLMOTT – **married** JANE COLES b. 1826 Toddington unknown date of marriage.

Children of CHARLES WILLMOTT and JANE are:

2.5.5.1   WILLIAM WILLMOTT b. 1848 in Luton Hertfordshire. Married MARIA BARNES born in Hockcliffe.

Children of WILLIAM WILLMOTT and MARIA are:

2.5.5.1.1 FREDERICK WILLMOTT b. 1871 Hitchen Hertfordshire d. 1927 **married** JANE PARSONS b. 1876
2.5.5.1.2 CLARA WILLMOTT b. 1874 Leighton Buzzard Bedfordshire. **Married** ROWLAND WHEELER b. 1872 in Husbourne Crawley Bedfordshire.
2.5.5.1.3 MILLY WILLMOTT b. 1888 Luton Hertfordshire
2.5.5.2   JANE WILLMOTT b. 1854 in Luton Hertfordshire

2.8.1 JOSEPH WILLMOTT *(HENRY(3), SAMUEL(2), EDWARD(1))* was born Abt. 1830 in Kings Walden Hertfordshire England. He married (1) SARAH GEARY ANDREWS. She was born Abt. 1834 in England. Daughter of Joseph Geary Andrews. He married (2) SARAH JONES. She was born Abt. 1841 in England.

Children of JOSEPH WILLMOTT and SARAH GEARY ANDREWS are:

2.8.1.1   HENRY WILLMOTT, b. 1858, Gt Berkhamsted. Hertfordshire.

2.8.1.2   LOUISA ANN GEARY WILLMOTT, b. 1859, Gt Berkhamsted, Hertfordshire.

2.8.1.3   JOSEPH GEARY WILLMOTT, b.1861, Gt Berkhamsted, Hertfordshire. (1881 census) visitor carpenters apprentice.

Children of JOSEPH WILLMOTT and SARAH JONES are:

2.8.1.4   MARGARET ELIZABETH WILLMOTT, b. Abt. 1869, Gt Berkhamsted, Hertfordshire.

2.8.1.5   JOHN EDWARD WILLMOTT, b. Abt. 1870, Gt Berkhamsted, Hertfordshire.

2.8.1.6   KATHERINE NANCY WILLMOTT, b. Abt. 1877, Gt Berkhamsted, Hertfordshire.

2.8.1.7   ARTHUR HERGEST WILLMOTT, b. Abt. 1875, Gt Berkharnsted, Hertfordshire.

2.8.1.8   ALBERT FRANK WILLMOTT, b. Abt. 1873, Gt Berkhamsted, Hertfordshire.

2.8.1.9   ALICE MAUD MARY WILLMOTT. b. Abt. 1872, Gt Berkhamsted, Hertfordshire

2.8.2   ELIZABETH ANN WILLMOTT *(HENRY (3), SAMUEL(2), EDWARD(1))* **was born** Abt. 1837 in Sandridge, Hertfordshire. She married JOHN WOOLSTON. He was born Abt. 1830 in Pirton Hertfordshire.

Children of ELIZABETH WILLMOTT and JOHN WOOLSTON are:

2.8.2.1   ELLEN LOUISA. WOOLSTON, b. Abt. 1861, Harpenden Hertfordshire.

2.8.2.2   HENRY JOHN WOOLSTON, b. Abt. 1863, Hexton Hertfordshire.

2.8.2.3   FREDERICK WILLIAM WOOLSTON, b. Abt. 1865, Hexton Hertfordshire.

2.8.2.4   ADELINE ELIZABETH WOOLSTON, b. Abt. 1866, Hexton Hertfordshire.

2.8.2.5   SARAH J WOOLSTON, b. Abt. 1869, Pegs down Bedfordshire.

2.8.2.6   FLORENCE MAUD WOOLSTON, b. Abt. 1871, Harpenden Hertfordshire.

2.8.2.7   MARY CHARLOTTE WOOLSTON, b. Abt. 1872, Harpenden Hertfordshire.

2.8.2.8   EVELYN LAVINIA WOOLSTON, b. Abt. 1874, Harpenden Hertfordshire.

2.8.2.9   HILDRED WOOLSTON, b. Abt. 1878, Harpenden Hertfordshire.

2.8.2.10   ARTHUR WILLMOTT WOOLSTON, b. Abt. Dec 1880, Harpenden Hertfordshire.

2.8.5   FREDERICK WILLMOTT, b. 18 Nov 1844, Harpenden Hertfordshire. (1881 census) Farmer 122 Act. Frederick married LAURA S.B.? She was 34 at the time of the 1881 census unknown DOB.

Children of FREDERICK WILLMOTT and LAURA are:

2.8.5.1   FRANCES L WILLMOTT, b. about 1869. (1881 census) 12yo Scholar
2.8.5.2   ETHEL L WILLMOTT, b about 1872. (1881 census) 9yo Scholar
2.8.5.3   HOPE G WILLMOTT, b about 1876. (1881 census) 5yo
2.8.5.4   IVY DOROTHY WILLMOTT, b 1881. (1881 census) 3mth old
2.8.5.5   REGINALD F WILLMOTT, b about 1880. (1881 census) 1yo
2.8.5.6   VIOLET N WILLMOTT, b about 1877. (1881 CENSUS) 4yo

2.8.9   HENRY WILLMOTT *(HENRY(3), SAMUEL(2), EDWARD(1))* **was born** Abt. 1832 in Kings Walden Hertfordshire England. He married ESTHER ?. She was born Abt. 1830 in England. Henry was a farmer in Harpenden. (1881 census)

Children of HENRY WILLMOTT and ESTHER? are:

2.8.9.1   LOUISA WILLMOTT, b. Abt. 1861, Harpenden Hertfordshire. (1881 Census) Farmer's Daughter

2.8.9.2   EMILY WILLMOTT, b. Abt. 1863, Harpenden Hertfordshire. (1881 Census) Farmer's Daughter

2.8.9.3   ANNIE WILLMOTT, b. Abt. 1864, Harpenden Hertfordshire. (1881 Census) Farmer's Daughter

2.8.9.4   ARTHUR WILLMOTT, b. Abt. 1868, Harpenden Hertfordshire. (1881 Census) Scholar

2.8.9.5   EDWARD WILLMOTT, b. Abt. 1866, Harpenden Hertfordshire. (1881 Census) Scholar

2.8.9.6   ESTHER WILLMOTT, b. Abt. 1870, Harpenden Hertfordshire. (1881 Census) Scholar

2.8.9.7   HARRIETT WILLMOTT, b. Abt. 1872, Harpenden Hertfordshire. (1881 Census) Scholar

2.8.9.8   ROBERT WILLMOTT, b. Abt. 1875, Harpenden Hertfordshire. (1881 Census) Scholar yo

2.8.1.3   JOSEPH GEARY WILLMOTT, b.1861, Gt Berkhamsted, Hertfordshire. Married SARAH CHENNELL who died in 1894 – buried in Boxmoor in Hertfordshire. He married a second time as well to Isabella Ratcliffe. His first wife died during childbirth to their 3rd child. They were raised by Joseph's family as he went off to sea.

Children of JOSEPH and SARAH CHENNELL

2.8.1.3.1   SARAH LOUISE GEARY WILLMOTT, b. 1881 Hemel
2.8.1.3.2   NELLIE WILLMOTT, 1884 Hemel
2.8.1.3.3   UNKNOWN FEMALE WILLMOTT, 1884

Children of JOSEPH and ISABELLA RATCLIFFE

2.8.1.3.4   ALICE WILLMOTT, born 1884.
2.8.1.3.5   REGINALD WILLMOTT, born 1896 Watford
2.8.1.3.6   GLADYS WILLMOTT, born 1899 Watford

2.8.1.3.4 ALICE WILLMOTT, born 1884 married GEORGE CHANDLER, born 1886 unknown where they were married.

Children of ALICE and GEORGE CHANDLER

2.8.1.3.4.1   DENNIS CHANDLER, born 1907
2.8.1.3.4.2   DORIS CHANDLER, born 1908, married PATRICK BRENTNALL
2.8.1.3.4.3   HARRY CHANDLER, born 1910, married ADELAIDE PIGGOTT
2.8.1.3.4.4   OLIVE CHANDLER, born 1916, married FREDERICK CHAPMAN

<u>*Australian Generations*</u>

1 SAMUEL CHARLES WILLMOTT *(SAMUEL (3), SAMUEL(2), EDWARD(1))* **was born** Abt. Apr 1837 **in Kings Walden Hertfordshire**, **and** he died 4 November 1894 of morbis cordus at Scot St Woods Point after an illness of 2 months, Samuel was a miner and engine driver. He married ELIZABETH DAVIS 28 Sep 1871 in Woods Point Victoria, daughter of MICHAEL DAVIS and MARY WATKINS. She was born 24 Dec 1845 in Melbourne, Victoria. After Samuel's death, Elizabeth moved to run a boarding house in Healesville. Samuel was the first family member from this line of descendants to migrate to Australia. He emigrated to NSW from Plymouth England in 1857 aboard the

Walter Morice which arrived in Sydney on 12 February 1849. Records state that he was 36yo we believe he lied to get onboard.

Children of SAMUEL WILLMOTT and ELIZABETH DAVIS are:

1.1   JOSEPH WILLMOTT, b. Abt. 1874, Woods Point Victoria.

1.2   EDWARD WILLMOTT, b. Abt. 1876, Woods Point Victoria, Moved to Kalgoorlie for the gold rush and remained and died Perth WA on 10 Feb 1920.

1.3   AMY ELIZABETH WILLMOTT, b. Abt. 1879, Woods Point Victoria.

1.4   JULIA WILLMOTT, b. 1881, Woods Point Victoria.

1.5   CHARLES HENRY WILLMOTT *(SAMUEL CHARLES(4), SAMUEL(3), SAMUEL92), EDWARD(1))* was born 23 Feb 1885 in Woods Point Victoria, and died 13th August 1958 buried in Cheltenham Cemetery.

1.6   WILLIAM THOMAS WILLMOTT *(SAMUEL CHARLES (4), SAMUEL(3), SAMUEL(2), EDWARD(1))* was born 07 Apr 1883 in Woods Point Victoria, and died 12 Oct 1957 in Moorabbin Victoria buried Brighton.

1.7   SAMUEL CHARLES WILLMOTT, b. 17 Jul 1872, Woods Point Victoria and died 15 Mar 1933 in Western Australia

1.5   CHARLES HENRY WILLMOTT *(SAMUEL CHARLES(4), SAMUEL(3), SAMUEL92), EDWARD(1))* was born 23 Feb 1885 in Woods Point Victoria, and died 13th August 1958 buried in Cheltenham Cemetery. He married (1) MARGARET JANE WHIGHT. He married (2) GRACE ELIZABETH PADBURY on 5th November 1912.

Child of CHARLES WILLMOTT and MARGARET WHIGHT is:

1.5.1   FREDERICK SAMUEL Willmott. Unknown date and place. D: 08 Nov 1973.

Children of CHARLES and GRACE ELIZABETH

1.5.2   FAITH WILLMOTT, b. 11th March 1915 in Hawthorn Victoria

1.5.3   CHARLES HENRY, b. 21st October 1913 Hawthorn Victoria

1.5.4   RUTH MARY, b. 3rd August 1921 in Hawthorn Victoria

1.7   SAMUEL CHARLES WILLMOTT, b. 17 Jul 1872, Woods Point Victoria and died 15 Mar 1933 in Western Australia. He married MARTHA FRIEND,

Abt. April 1896 in Gippsland, Victoria. Samuel moved to Kalgoorlie with his brothers for the gold rush, he stayed on and died in WA. Martha passed away February 1950 Perth Western Australia.

Children of SAMUEL CHARLES WILLMOTT and MARTHA FRIEND are:

1.7.1   SAMUEL WILLMOTT, b. 14 February 1898 in Woods Point died 10 May 1898 due to bronchitis.

1.7.2   MARTHA VICTORIA WILLMOTT, b. 1899 in Woods Point, d. 1 January 1987 Perth Western Australia

1.7.3   EDWARD WILLMOTT, b. 1897 in Woods Point, d.22 August 1978 Perth Western Australia

1.7.4   VICTORIA WILLMOTT, b. 1899 Woods Point Victoria

1.7.5   LIVING WILLMOTT

1.7.6   RUTH ELIZABETH WILLMOTT, b.9 December 1902 Kanowna Western Australia, d. 4 September 1984 Fremantle Western Australia.

1.6   WILLIAM THOMAS WILLMOTT *(SAMUEL CHARLES (4), SAMUEL(3), SAMUEL(2), EDWARD(1))* was born 07 Apr 1883 in Woods Point Victoria, and died 12 Oct 1957 in Moorabbin Victoria buried Brighton. He married (1) MARY EDWARDS. He married (2) OLIVE MAY BEST 13 Jan 1915 in Northcote Victoria, daughter of MARTRA STEEVINS PARFREY. She was born 15 Jan 1891, and died Abt. 1922 in Brighton Victoria. William went with his brothers to WA but returned and married.

Children of WILLLIAM WILLMOTT and MARY EDWARDS are:

1.6.1   ISABEL WILLMOTT. B. Abt Mar 1927 Died 6 June 1927 at 3mths old approx

1.6.2   KENNETH WILLMOTT **was born** 6 June 1928 **in Melbourne Victoria**. Died May 1998.

Children of WILLIAM WILLMOTT and OLIVE BEST are:

1.6.3   MYRTLE DILYS WILLMOIT *(WILLIAM THOMAS(5), SAMUEL CHARLES(4), SAMUEL(3), SAMUEL(2), EDWARD(1))* was born 04 Sep 1915 in Melbourne Victoria.

1.6.4   ROY WILLMOTT *(WILLLIAM* THOMAS(5), *SAMUEL CHARLES(4), SAMUEL(3), SAMUEL(2) EDWARD(1))* was born 08 Sep 1917 in Melbourne Victoria, and died 24 May 1966 in Melbourne Victoria.

1.6.5   SAMUEL WILLIAM WILLMOTT *(WILLIAM THOMAS(5), SAMUEL CHARLES (4), SAMUEL(3), SAMUEL(2) EDWARD(1))* was born 24 Jan 1919 in Ripponlea.

1.6.6   ALLAN WILLMOTT *(WILLIAM THOMAS(5), SAMUEL CHARLES(4), SAMUEL(3), SAMUEL(2), EDWARD(1))* was born 17 Nov 1921 in Melbourne Victoria.

1.6.2   KENNETH WILLMOTT **was born** 6 June 1928 **in Melbourne Victoria**. Died May 1998. **He first married** JULIE AUDREY WEBB 19 Dec 1953 **she was born** 19 Dec 1937 **in Prahran Victoria. He secondly married** FLORA MAY MURRAY 24 May 1969

Children of KENNETH WILLMOTT and JULIE AUDREY WEBB are:

1.6.2.1   GLENDA ISABEL WILLMOTT **was born** 29 April 1954 **in Caulfield Victoria.**
1.6.2.2   WENDY JANE WILLMOTT **was born** 24 November 1957 in Springvale Victoria

1.6.2.3   DARYL FRASER WILLMOTT **was born** 1 June 1962 in Dandenong Victoria.

Child of KENNETH WILLMOTT and FLORA MAY MURRAY is:

1.6.2.4   RODERICK KENNETH WILLMOTT **was born** 10 March 1970, Adopted son of Flora and Kenneth.

1.6.3   MYRTLE DILYS WILLMOIT *(WILLIAM THOMAS(5),* SAMUEL *CHARLES(4), SAMUEL(3), SAMUEL(2), EDWARD(1))* was born 04 Sep 1915 in Melbourne Victoria. She married RUSSELL STRONG. Possibly still residing in Eildon VIC

Child of MYRTLE WILLMOTT and RUSSELL STRONG is:

6.3.1   GRAHAM STRONG, b. not known.

1.6.4   ROY WILLMOTT *(WILLLIAM* THOMAS(5), *SAMUEL CHARLES(4), SAMUEL(3), SAMUEL(2) EDWARD(1))* was born 08 Sep 1917 in Melbourne Victoria, and died 24 May 1966 in Melbourne Victoria. He married VERA

STEELE, daughter of WILLIAM STEELE and SARAH AHERN. She was born 24 May 1917 in Melbourne Victoria, and died 16 Jan 1989 in Albury NSW buried Springvale.

Children of Roy WILLMOTT and VERA STEELE are:

1.6.4.1 DENNIS *ROY WILLMOTT* (ROY (6), *WILLLIAM THOMAS* (5), *SAMUEL CHARLES (4), SAMUEL (3), SAMUEL (2) EDWARD (1))* was born 12 Jul 1943 in Elsternwick
1.6.4.2 BARBARA EVELYN WILLMOTT, b. 12th March 1946 Elsternwick died. 16th March 1946 at 4 days old buried at Brighton cemetery

1.6.4.3 HELEN WILLMOTT (ROY (6), *WILLLIAM THOMAS* (5), *SAMUEL CHARLES (4), SAMUEL (3), SAMUEL (2) EDWARD (1)) was* born 26 Sep 1947 in Elsternwick.

1.6.5 SAMUEL WILLIAM WILLMOTT *(WILLIAM THOMAS(5), SAMUEL CHARLES (4), SAMUEL(3), SAMUEL(2) EDWARD(1))* was born 24 Jan 1919 in Ripponlea. He married VIDA DANIELS. He died 24 Mar 1982 in Queensland.

Children of SAMUEL WILLMOTT and VIDA DANIELS are:

1.6.5.1 JOHN WILLMOTT, b. 25 November 1945.
1.6.5.2 GARRY WILLMOTT (QLD), b. 1 January 1952.

1.6.6 ALLAN WILLMOTT *(WILLIAM THOMAS(5), SAMUEL CHARLES(4), SAMUEL(3), SAMUEL(2), EDWARD(1))* was born 17 Nov 1921 in Melbourne Victoria. He married MARGARET DORMAND, b. 2 March unknown year d. 27 March 1976. Allan and Margaret met in a hospital where she was working as a nurse. They possibly ran a motel in Albury/Wodonga in the 1970's. Allan has possibly remarried.

Children of ALLAN WILLMOTT and MARGARET DORMAND are:

1.6.6.1 ROBERT WILLMOTT **was born** 17 July late 1940s
1.6.6.2 DOROTHY WILLMOTT, 27th December late 1940s

1.6.6.3 PETER WILLMOTT, unknown dob

1.6.6.4 DAVID WILLMOTT, b. 26 April late 1950s

1.6.6.5 JOHN WILLMOTT, b. 13 March 1952

1.1.6.1 GLENDA ISABEL WILLMOTT **was born** 29 April 1954 **in Caulfield Victoria. She married** JOSEPH OTTAWAY **born** 28 March 1956 in Rockhampton. They married January 1983 in Brisbane.

Children of GLENDA ISABEL and JOSEPH OTTAWAY are:

1.6.2.1.1 KATE BAYLY OTTAWAY, b. 26.April 1980

1.6.2.1.2 TIMOTHY JAMES OTTAWAY, b. 25 August 1984

1.6.2.1.3 CHRISTOPHER THOMAS OTTAWAY, b. 8 September 1987

1.1.6.2 WENDY JANE WILLMOTT **was born** 24 November 1957 in Springvale Victoria. She never married but had children to GORDON BYRON, b. 9 July 1956 in Glasglow.

Children of WENDY JANE WILLMOTT and GORDON BYRON are:

1.1.6.2.1 CLAIR JADE BYRON, b 4 October 1981 in Sydney
1.1.6.2.2 JOANNE AMBER BYRON, b. 27 May 1986 Sydney

1.1.6.3 DARYL FRASER WILLMOTT **was born** 1 June 1962 in Dandenong Victoria. **He married** LEONIE SANDERSON, b. 9 May 1978 in Queensland. They married in December 1999.

Children of DARYL FRASER WILLMOTT and LEONIE SANDERSON are:

6.2.2.1 NOAH WILLMOTT, b. 22 January 2002 in Brisbane
6.2.2.2 ELIJAH WILLMOTT, b. 19 September 2005 in Brisbane.

1.6.4.1 DENNIS *ROY WILLMOTT* (ROY (6), *WILLLIAM THOMAS* (5), *SAMUEL CHARLES (4), SAMUEL (3), SAMUEL (2) EDWARD (1))* was born 12 Jul 1943 in Elsternwick He married (1) MARION ELIZABETH MCKENZIE 08 Apr 1965 in Bentleigh Victoria, daughter of KENNETH MCKENZIE and JEAN CARTER. She was horn 23 May 1944 in Melbourne Victoria. (2) SANDRA?

Children of DENNIS WILLMOTT and MARION MCKENZIE are:

1.6.4.1.1 PETER ROY WILLMOTT *(DENNIS ROY(7)*, ROY(6), *WILLLIAM THOMAS(5), SAMUEL CHARLES(4),SAMUEL(3), SAMUEL(2) EDWARD(1))* was born *26 Apr 1967* in Ferntree *Gully Victoria*

1.6.4.1.2   DANIELLE NICOLE WILLMOTT, b. 08 Apr 1969, Ferntree Gully Victoria; m. MATHEW COPLIN,

10 Sep 2005, Footscray.

1.6.4.1.3 REBEKAH MICHELLE WILLMOTT, b. 13 Sep 1974, Ferntree Gully Victoria.

1.6.4.2   HELEN WILLMOTT (ROY (6), *WILLLIAM THOMAS* (5), *SAMUEL CHARLES (4), SAMUEL (3), SAMUEL (2) EDWARD (1)) was* born 26 Sep 1947 in Elsternwick. She married LYLE ALLEN.

Children of HELEN WILLMOTT and LYLE ALLEN are:

1.6.4.2.1 JODY ALLEN *(HELEN(7) WILLMOTT*, ROY(6), *WILLLIAM THOMAS(5), SAMUEL CHARLES(4), SAMUEL(3), SAMUEL(2) EDWARD(1))* was born *22 Sep 1971* in Melbourne Victoria. She married RODNEY BENNETT.
1.6.4.2.2 KYLIE ALLEN, b. 1973, Melbourne Victoria; m. SID FERNANDO.

1.6.5.1   JOHN WILLMOTT, b. 25 November 1940. Married twice, he first married Gail Wright then he remarried Valerie unknown surname.

Children of JOHN WILLMOTT and GAIL WRIGHT are:

1.6.5.1.1   LISA WILLMOTT

1.6.5.1.2   ANTHONY WILLMOTT

1.6.5.3 GARRY WILLMOTT (7)
Married ELIZABETH ANNE WEBSTER b. 1 March 1954

Married ANNA LOUISE SHEARER 2nd July 1996

Children of GARRY WILLMOTT and first wife are:

1.6.5.2.1 EMMA LOUISE WILLMOTT, b. 3 July 1982

1.6.5.2.2 SOPHIE JANE WILLMOTT, b. 14 December 1984

1.6.6.1   ROBERT WILLMOTT **was born** 17 July late 40s. He married a lady unknown name

Children of ROBERT WILLMOTT and wife are:

1.6.6.1.1 DARIEN WILLMOTT – 3 children

1.6.6.1.2 LISA WILLMOTT – 2 children

1.6.6.1.3 TINA WILLMOTT – 2 children

1.6.4.1.1 PETER ROY(8) WILLMOTT *(DENNIS ROY(7)*, ROY(6), *WILLLIAM* THOMAS(5), *SAMUEL*

CHARLES(4), SAMUEL(3), SAMUEL(2) EDWARD(1)) was born *26 Apr 1967* in Ferntree *Gully Victoria.*

He married DIANNE ALOE *17* Jan *1987* in Mentone Victoria. She was born *08* Jul *1963* in Sydney.

Children of PETER WILLMOTT *and* DIANNE ALOE are:

1.6.4.1.1.1 ANDREW JOHN(9) WILLMOTT, b. 06 Jun 1989, Frankston Victoria.(Twin)

1.6.4.1.1.2 MICHAEL ROY WILLMOTT, b. 06 Jun 1989, Frankston Victoria. (Twin)

1.6.4.1.1.3 WILLIAM TRAE WILLMOTT, b. 17 Jun 1996, Wodonga Victoria.

1.6.4.2.1 JODY ALLEN *(HELEN(7) WILLMOTT,* ROY(6), *WILLLIAM* THOMAS(5), *SAMUEL CHARLES(4), SAMUEL(3), SAMUEL(2) EDWARD(1))* was born *22* Sep *1971* in Melbourne Victoria.

Children *of* JODY ALLEN and RODNEY BENNETT are:

1.6.4.2.1.1 TIAGEN BENNETT, b. 20 Feb 1996, Melbourne Victoria.

1.6.4.2.1.2 JARROD BENNETT, b. 25 Mar 1999, Melbourne Victoria.

1.6.4.1.2 DANIELLE NICOLE WILLMOTT, b. 08 Apr 1969, Ferntree Gully Victoria; m. MATHEW COPLIN, 10 Sep 2005, Footscray.

Children *of* Danielle and Mathew:

1.6.4.1.2 .1 ZACHARY ROY COPELAND, b. 2 June 2006 Melbourne

1.6.4.1.2 .2 MADDISON BETH COPELAND, b. 2 June 2006 Melbourne

Daniel Vida's family Tree

Vida Louisa Willmott b 1920 Northcote Victoria

M 6th June Brighton Victoria

Harry Daniel b 23rd April 1876 Illabarook Victoria m 18th August 1896

Stevedore

Jane Iffinger b 19th September 1879 South Melbourne

Housemaid

James Daniel b 1847 St Ives Cornwell England m 3rd November 1873 Ballarat Victoria

Miner

Angelina Hadler b 1852

Richard Iffinger b 1854 Heidelberg Germany m 1st June 1877 Port Melbourne

Jane Turner b 22nd October 1859 St Kilda Victoria m 1st June

James Daniel estimated b1820

Johanna Quick b 1824

William Hadler b 1807 Kent England m 1851

Eliza Williams b 1838 Windsor NSW

Conrad Iffinger b 1824 Heidelberg Germany

Baebara Khestal b Germany

James Turner b 1819 Leith Scotland

Emily Harriet 1819 Leith Scotland

First published 2024 by Crabtree Pty Ltd

All rights reserved.

No part of this publication may be reproduced, stored in a retrieval system, or transmitted in any form or any means electronic, mechanical, photocopying, recording or otherwise without the prior permission of the publisher.

Copyright © Crabtree Pty Ltd 2024

ISBN: 978-0-6459087-2-5 (p/b)
ISBN: 978-0-6459087-3-2 (ebook)

www.ingramcontent.com/pod-product-compliance
Lightning Source LLC
LaVergne TN
LVHW091552070426
835507LV00010B/804